Getting Your Life Under Control

Making Order From The Chaos

Kristen Kansiewicz

All stories and case examples contained in this book are fictional representations. All names and case details have been significantly altered to protect the privacy of any individuals upon which the story themes were based.

All websites or resources listed in this book were available at the time of this publication and may be subject to change. The resources are listed as suggestions but do not necessarily represent a full endorsement by the author.

Getting Your Life Under Control
Copyright © 2014 Kristen Kansiewicz
All rights reserved.

Cover photo: gwolters/Shutterstock
Cover design: Heather Cahill

ISBN: 1-494-99577-8
ISBN-13: 978-1-494-99577-5

To my clients, who have worked so hard to move towards healing in their lives. May you continue to be an inspiration to me and to others.

Contents

ACKNOWLEDGMENTS

PREFACE   *1*

INTRODUCTION   *3*

1.   AREAS OF LIFE MANAGEMENT   *7*
2.   WHAT IS A SYSTEM?   *15*
3.   FINDING THE ROOT   *33*
4.   MAKING CHANGES   *43*
5.   THE ROADMAP TO STABILITY   *57*
6.   TASK & TIME MANAGEMENT   *67*
7.   RELATIONSHIP MANAGEMENT   *77*
8.   MONEY MANAGEMENT   *91*
9.   ADDICTIONS   *103*
10.   ACHIEVING LIFE GOALS   *113*
11.   MAINTAINING YOUR VICTORY   *123*

Acknowledgments

A huge thank you to my husband, Joshua, for his support in making this project happen. You continually challenge me and inspire me to do big things.

Thank you to Pastor Kurt Lange for his support and guidance as I grow spiritually and professionally.

A big round of applause to my team of editors: Becky Miller, Kimberly Hogsett, Bob Leppanen, and my mother, Linda Bennett, as well as graphics editor Heather Cahill. Thank you for helping me make this book great!

I am truly blessed by God to serve in His kingdom and am grateful for His investment in me. May I be faithful to the work He has for me.

Preface

Before you begin this book, I need to warn you about a few things.

First, I do not think you should read this book if you are not open to changing yourself or your life in significant ways. This book is for people who are tired of the status quo and who don't want to live one more day in chaos. You do not have to be ready to change all at once (chapters 4 and 5 will walk you through the process of change that lasts), but you do need to be open to the idea.

Second, you are going to need some type of notebook or journal along with a pen next to you while reading this book. (I have included a few blank pages at the end of the book for notes in case you are without a journal.) If you want this book to change your life (which I certainly believe it has the potential to do), you cannot skim or speed read. In fact, I will often tell you to pause or re-read a previous section. This book is meant to be digested, discussed with a friend or mentor, and wrestled with. You may even want to read it several times. I hope that these pages are wrinkled, dog-eared, and tear-stained when you are done.

Finally, you need to know that right from the start I will be encouraging you to develop a relationship with Jesus. It is my firm belief that true and lasting change comes from experiencing God's forgiveness, grace, and love for you. I am a professional Christian counselor and I write from a Christian perspective, so if that offends you, know that you have been duly warned.

I consider this book a launching point: you will get out of it what you put in. The resources I recommend throughout the book are just to get you started; there are many other wonderful resources out there. I do not endorse every word of every book listed, but I am confident there is good to be found for those who can read with a critical eye.

This book represents thousands of conversations I have had with clients through my more than twelve years in the mental health field. I have given almost all of this advice in bits and pieces, and I have walked many clients down the road you are about to undertake. I know that the principles in this book can change lives, and I hope that yours is next.

Introduction

If you have chosen to pick up this book right now, chances are there is something in your life that feels out of control. You might use words like "chaotic" or "unmanageable" to describe how your life feels to you. When you look at your life, you see a giant mess and even just knowing where to start fixing it is overwhelming.

My dad always said that when facing a problem the first step is to admit the problem. While this may sound somewhat obvious, in life we often try to cover up, ignore, or fix a problem without first acknowledging that we have a problem. Denial of problems is often a coping strategy we have learned. Admitting the problem means taking a look at yourself. Guilt, shame, anger, depression, and a host of other complicated feelings can stop us from being able to tolerate looking at ourselves.

If you want to address the problems of a chaotic life, you have to start somewhere. You cannot wait until you no longer feel shame or guilt. You cannot wait until life becomes more calm (because order does not spring up from chaos). You can choose to wait until you hit rock bottom, but do you really want your life to get worse before trying to get better?

You have a choice. Right here, right now. You can keep going the way you've been going. Put this book down right now and say, "I can't do it." Or you can admit the problem: "I cannot manage my own life." Those with an addiction recovery background may recognize this as Step 1. Across a wide variety of problems, this is a good place to start.

One key aspect to admitting that you are unable to manage your life is to look to something outside yourself for help. Some have called this the "Higher Power" – someone who CAN control your life. In this quest to turn over our lives to someone bigger, we must pursue truth, not merely a reality we create in our minds.

I have personally chosen to study the Bible along with books of other faiths and have found truth in the claims of Jesus. More than just a man, Jesus was fully divine and lives today. In my surrender of my life to Jesus Christ, I have found peace and hope beyond my own abilities and circumstances.

It is my hope that you will begin this journey for a well-managed life outside yourself. Before we begin to take practical steps towards change, we must recognize our own powerlessness to do so by ourselves. If you have not read the Bible, put this book down and start with that instead. Get to know Jesus through the Gospels of Mark or Luke. Find a local church that can help you explore your questions and understand how to surrender to God.

If you have already surrendered your life to God but are still having problems with a chaotic life, this book is for you. Surrender is the first step, but there are many other steps towards growth and change. Keep reading as we journey together to discover areas of your life that may be out of control as well as discovering the root issues causing the chaos in your life.

1

AREAS OF LIFE MANAGEMENT

In this chapter, we will explore some of the areas in life that can become chaotic. Later on we will discuss things that lead to disruption in these areas, but let's start with simply identifying which areas of your life feel out of control.

TASKS

Perhaps the most outwardly visible way your life can get out of control is in the area of tasks. You have a household or work task to do and you simply cannot accomplish it without something going wrong. Usually people who struggle with managing tasks are very well-intentioned and truly want to follow through.

Let's take a look at Sheri, who struggles with managing tasks in her life. A 36-year-old mother of two, Sheri would like to say that her children are the cause of her inability to keep her house clean, but deep down she knows that she has never been able to manage tasks well. The laundry is always in the washing machine, but it hardly ever makes it to the dryer before the wet clothes have sat for a few days. At work, Sheri feels like she ends every day with loose ends rather than finished projects. The ones she does finish end up feeling like the least important tasks.

TIME

Another area of life that can often become out of control is time management. Problems with time management and task management often go together, but not always. When you are struggling with time management, you may feel like you are able to accomplish all your tasks, but not in the time frame you needed to. Frequently you are running late because you accomplished too many tasks, rather than not enough. You may play games with the clock, almost racing against it to see how much you can squeeze in and only be "a little late."

Bill shares your struggle. The classic extrovert, Bill loves people and loves the spotlight. At a party, he is the center who knows everybody there. The party doesn't start until Bill arrives, which is usually at least half an hour late. In that setting, his friends don't seem to mind. But when they make plans to get to a show and Bill is late (again), his friends begin to get frustrated. They just don't feel they can trust Bill or rely on him to be there when he says he will. Bill feels frustrated with himself because he hates letting people down, but there always seems to be someone who needs his help or one last project that needs to be wrapped up. He feels that he really just doesn't know how to be on time.

Relationships

Some readers may feel encouraged so far, thinking, "I feel like I can get things done and I am usually on time... Maybe my life isn't chaotic after all..." But life management isn't only about getting tasks done or keeping a schedule. Your relationships matter too, and sometimes relationship chaos is one of the areas that feels the most unmanageable. Why? Because in a relationship there is another person's behavior that you cannot control. How are you supposed to decrease the chaos in your relationships if the other people in your life are just as chaotic as you? You struggle with chaos in this area if you find yourself frequently in conflict with others, if you find that "drama" has a way of finding you, or if your friends/family pull you back into negative patterns in your life.

Jocelyn struggles with managing her relationships. She would describe herself as a compassionate person who is always willing to help others. Just last month, a "close" friend (whom she met two weeks prior) was in a crisis because her housing was in jeopardy. Of course Jocelyn said the friend could move in with her for a while – surely she could not be mean enough to let her friend live in the streets! The friend said it would only be a few days, but a month later

Jocelyn is wondering how long this will last. She can't take much more because she is already stressed from the arguments she keeps having on the phone with her mother. Maybe she'll get lucky and her mother will stop speaking to her (again)...

Money

Ahh, the "M" word... makes the world go 'round, right? Yet when money management is a problem in your life, it seems there's never enough of it to go around. If you find yourself rotating bills that you put off each month, are racking up more and more credit card debt, or find yourself borrowing from friends just to scrape by, you have a problem with money management. There are many root causes for chaos in the financial area of your life, and we will discuss these later. The most important concept to grasp right now is this: your problem will not be fixed by having more money. When impaired money management is creating chaos in your life, the problem only gets worse when you have more money.

Take Sam, for example. He makes $70,000 per year and has a wife and one child. Some would say this is more than enough to live on. But not Sam. He has $20,000 of credit card debt (built up over the past 10 years), a large mortgage on a house that he can no longer sell because he owes more than it is worth, he has a car payment of $500 per month (in a lease that he agreed to while on an impulse stop at a car dealership), and he finds he eats lunch out most days because he doesn't have time to grab something before he leaves the house in the morning. Sam finds himself daydreaming at work about getting a big bonus because then he could REALLY afford to live. A vintage Mustang convertible would really help him relax on weekends...

ADDICTIONS

Before you are too quick to skip this section, pause for a moment to assess your life. Addictions are not just about alcohol and drugs. Certainly those are addictive and a common problem. But there are many other areas of addiction as well: shopping, pornography/sex, prescriptions, technology (including use of phones, computers, tablets, video games, etc.), and gambling to name a few.

Any life-controlling habit is an addiction. You are out of control because you cannot stop. You may have even convinced yourself that "it's not that bad" or that you could stop if you "wanted to." This area of life can overlap all of the other areas previously mentioned, as it takes away from your ability to accomplish tasks, disrupts your time, harms your relationships, drains your financial resources, and prevents you from moving forward on any life goals.

Jimmy is an addict, but not one you'd pick out of a crowd. Jimmy drinks occasionally, but never gets drunk. He has never used drugs and doesn't smoke. He holds down a job (although he isn't advancing as fast as he thought he would) and while he may miss a bill or two now and then, he manages his money fairly well. Acquaintances of Jimmy's would never guess that he struggles with an addiction, but his close friends and family are beginning to see just how serious his problem is. Jimmy is addicted to video gaming. He doesn't just enjoy playing in his free time; he HAS to play. It started as just a way to unwind after work, but soon Jimmy became obsessed with beating every level and then beating his own best scores. Instead of playing for an hour or two, Jimmy finds himself getting on at 7pm or so and staying on until 2 or 3 in the morning. He is often tired at work because he's just not getting enough sleep anymore. When he does close his eyes, all he sees is the game. Recently his addiction has become so strong that he finds himself thinking about gaming throughout his day, dreaming up ideas for ways to beat a challenging level or looking on the internet for new games to try. Even Jimmy is starting to feel a little out of control.

LIFE GOALS

For some, day to day life seems to be manageable. You have a daily routine that is pretty stable, you manage your time and tasks well, and while you don't make a lot of money you feel like you are making ends meet. Yet something still feels off because you just don't feel like you can ever get ahead in life. You have dreams and goals, but in some ways your routine seems to get in the way. "Chaos" might not describe you, yet your life feels very out of your control. Maybe you thought that you'd be in a different place in life by your age. Maybe you thought you'd really go places, though you were not sure where.

In the movie *It's a Wonderful Life*, we see a great example of someone who has trouble managing his life goals. Jimmy Stewart plays George Bailey: a responsible, hard-working oldest son who always planned to go to college, move away, and get out of his "crummy town." Yet every time he plans to leave, he is held back by responsibilities weighing on him. Despite his determination that he would never do so, he takes over the family Savings & Loan. The business gets down to the last dollar, his life isn't what he thought it would be, and he contemplates suicide. With the help of his guardian angel and a supportive town coming to his aid, George begins to see some hope. Unfortunately, not all of us have an angel at our doorstep and a small town coming to our house to bail us out our problems. This area of life management is perhaps the most discouraging when it feels out of control.

If you have identified one or more areas of your life that are out of control, make sure you have started with step one: admit the problem. Admit it to yourself, perhaps by writing it down, and admit it aloud to one trusted friend or family member. Admit it to God and take a moment to pray, asking Him to help you in this area. Make a commitment to follow God's commands in the Bible as a foundation for your life.

Once you have taken this step, you will be ready to continue on to the next step: finding the root cause. Finding the root problem is no easy task, and we must start by broadening our understanding of what causes your problems to happen over and over again. If your life has a pattern of chaos, you will need to take a step back and look at the bigger picture of your life.

In the next chapter, we will explore the concept of a system (your chaos is bigger than just you!) and explore systems that contribute to an out of control life. Understanding the concept of systems will help us go deeper towards the root of the problem as well as give us strategies for change.

2

WHAT IS A SYSTEM?

Some people just love to get their hands dirty. (I am not necessarily one of those people...) You know the type, maybe you are one of them. The true gardener: connected with the soil and able to get a seed to grow just about anywhere.

Whether or not you have a green thumb, you need dirt. Some quick internet research tells you all you need to know:

> To understand what goes on in the soil, we first need a short introduction into what it contains. In short, soil is a mixture of rock particles, minerals, organic material and living organisms. All of these soil components team up to form a fascinating ecosystem, and one of the bases of all life on Earth. Without rich soil, we couldn't have plants, or animals or humans.[1]

---

[1] McArthur, Yvonne. "Dirt: The Incredible Ecosystem Beneath Our Feet." Environmental Graffiti. 12/2012. Web. 12/18/2013.

Without dirt, you wouldn't be alive right now.

So what does dirt have to do with getting your life under control? Is gardening the secret to an orderly life? Of course not. But a look into the ecosystems of the earth can help us understand relational systems too. Just as a small impact on an environmental ecosystem can bring chaos to a species, so too can small decisions make big impacts on the delicate balance of your life.

Let's take a look at some of the systems you have in your life right now. First, you have a family system. Even if you are single living alone right now, you no doubt grew up in some kind of family system. Your family system may have been disconnected, dysfunctional, or disorderly, but it nonetheless was (and still is) a system that impacts you.

Another kind of system in your life is your social system. Your friends, church, social network, and even the places you go to have fun make up a system in your life. These relational surroundings are a very influential part of your life and can increase or decrease chaos. Take a minute to ask yourself, "Who do I spend time with? Where do I spend most of my time?" The answers to these questions may help you gain awareness of your social system.

In addition to your family and social systems, you also have your daily routine. I will call this your "self-care system." Your awareness of yourself is critical to make this system operational. You may be a person who is unaware of your own needs, in which case you are likely not providing yourself with enough self-care. A plant in need of lots of water will not thrive in a desert; neither will a person thrive without meeting his or her own physical and emotional needs.

The final system we will discuss in this chapter is an undercurrent to all the other systems: your value system. Your culture and your beliefs are the primary components of your value system, and these provide a framework for decision making that cannot be overstated. The direction your life will head is directly tied to your value system. The good news here if you are experiencing chaos in your life is that you can make changes in your value system. It is change in this system that can most significantly change your life.

Examining your life systems is absolutely critical in the process of change. You will not find the root of your life chaos without understanding how you have been shaped by these systems and how you can begin to make small decisions that impact your systems in big ways. So let's dig deeper now into each of these systems to explore common problems in each of these areas.

Family Systems

You were born into a family system over which you had no control. Generational patterns were set in motion before you had even arrived. Your parents have a history, their parents have a history, and so on. Your socioeconomic status, your perspective on life, and your social interactions all tie back to those histories.

Dr. Murray Bowen was the leading theorist who wrote and developed concepts of family systems in the 1970s. His work and theories continue to influence the training of counselors and family therapists.[2]

Bowen's theory outlined ways in which the family dynamic is created through various types of interactions. "Triangling," for example, is the idea that in a family sometimes three or more people are involved in managing each two-person relationship. Two siblings may have difficulty communicating, and their mother may become "triangled" into settling their conflicts. A worse situation is when two parents, whether married or divorced, "triangle" their children into their relationship to keep the peace.

Other Bowen concepts involve identification of stressors on the emotional life of the family, the impact of the emotional health of the parents on the children, ways in which patterns and systems are passed on generationally, independence or dependence among family

---

[2] For a more in-depth, academic read, check out the book *Bowen Theory and Practice* (3rd ed., 1997) available at www.thebowencenter.org or through independent sellers on Amazon.com as of 12/2013.

members, and even the impact of sibling order on your relational functioning.[3]

The framework Bowen laid was the foundation for language we now use every day when we talk about families. The word "dysfunctional" implies that there is something wrong or unhealthy. Bowen and many others in the field of family therapy have sought to create definitions for healthy and unhealthy family systems.

So what actually defines a healthy or a dysfunctional family? The answer you get to this question may vary depending on who you ask, but underlying themes in most answers will include basic interpersonal rules (such as respect for all family members), clear and open communication, emotional and physical safety, and an ability to resolve conflict effectively.

To explore your family system, ask yourself the following questions:

- How did my family respond to stress?
- How did my family handle conflict?
- How close was my family?
- What stressors did my family face?
- How did my family handle decision making, goal setting, and money?
- How did my family communicate with one another?
- Were drugs/alcohol present?

---

[3] http://www.thebowencenter.org/pages/theory.html

- Was abuse (physical, verbal, sexual) present?

Your life is very likely still impacted by the answers to those questions. Common family problems that often lead to family chaos include the following:

- *Extreme stress response:* Overreaction to stress (drama) or a lack of response (apathy or fear of acknowledgement) to stressors.
- *Extreme conflict response:* Intense, angry conflict or denial patterns in which conflict was ignored.
- *Extreme closeness or distance:* Overly close (codependent) relationships in which there was little freedom or very detached relationships in which anyone could come and go into or out of the system.
- *Extreme stressors:* Divorce, death, frequent moves or job changes, financial problems, or cultural discrimination.
- *Extreme decision making:* Dictatorship-style decisions or a lack of ability to make decisions among caregivers, lack of follow through or planning on family goals, or patterns of debt and money mismanagement.
- *Extreme communication:* Frequent yelling, name-calling, or accusing language; or silent treatment, leaving the house when

angry, withholding love, or other passive-aggressive behavior.
- *Addiction issues:* Presence of drug, alcohol, or other addiction in one or both caregivers.
- *Abuse issues:* Children being witness to domestic violence or being abused themselves.

This list is certainly not exhaustive, but it begins to help us reflect on our family dynamics. This awareness will be useful in identifying those same patterns in your life today.

Social Systems

Your family system was your first social system. As you grew up, you expanded this system by making friends, going to school, and increasing your independence outside the home. In a healthy and stable childhood, this independence and separation from family comes gradually. For some, stressors of all sorts contribute to sudden or early separation from family.

The closeness or bond you had with your early caregivers is called "attachment." Attachment theory was first developed in 1946 by John Bowlby.[4] He and his colleague Mary Ainsworth continued throughout their careers to

---

[4] Bowlby, J. (1946). *Maternal Care and Mental Health.* Geneva: World Health Organization.

study the impact of early childhood closeness to caregivers. Terms like "separation anxiety" are now part of everyday language, but in 1946 these were concepts yet to be developed.

Your attachment patterns directly impact your ability to form and keep relationships. Ainsworth identified three attachment styles:
- *Secure attachment:* a child is a little upset when the caregiver leaves but is able to play after a short period of time and is happy when the caregiver returns.
- *Resistant-insecure attachment:* a child is extremely upset when the caregiver leaves but resists the caregiver's affection upon return.
- *Avoidant-insecure attachment:* a child ignores the caregiver and does not show much emotion when the caregiver leaves or returns.[5]

How well (or poorly) you attached to your early caregivers has likely been repeated in your social relationships. Those who experienced a secure attachment learned to trust others. Those who had resistant relationships with caregivers may find as adolescents and adults that they have intense relationships that begin (and end) quickly. If you had avoidant attachment patterns, you may find yourself less interested in

---

[5] Ainsworth, M., Blehar, M., Waters, E., & Wall, S. (1978). *Patterns of Attachment.* Hillsdale, NJ: Erlbaum.

relationships in general and may have difficulty establishing close relationships.

In addition to thinking about your own attachment patterns, it is important to think about what supports you have in your social system now. Stop reading right now and make a list of your friends. Once you have done that, put a star by the names of people who help you move forward in your life. Next circle the names of people who have their own issues of dysfunction and chaos. Ask yourself, "How much time do I spend with those who help me? How much time do I spend with those who add chaos or drama into my life?"

Friends offer one kind of support, but your social system also needs connection with resources and groups. Churches, recovery groups, and counselors are often important parts of your social system. Other community resources, like a parenting class or a food pantry may be necessary for you as well.

People who are experiencing life chaos are likely to have cracks and holes in their social system. Their family and friend relationships, rather than offering support, actually increase conflict and disorder. This adds stress to life, leading to even more chaos.

Lack of access or unwillingness to access larger community groups is also a crack in the social system. Sadly, sometimes these groups have their own systemic chaos so that even when there is access it does not offer help to you. In addition, there may be groups you are a part of (such as a gang or a favorite bar crowd) that have a negative impact on your life.

The following are some questions that can help you identify root problems tied to your social system:
- How many friends do I have? Do they help or harm me?
- Do I isolate or withdraw when I am having a hard time?
- Do I have difficulty forming or keeping relationships?
- What groups am I part of? Do I feel like I belong?
- Where do I spend my time? Are these places safe and orderly or is there chaos present?
- Are there resources I need that I don't know how to access or I am afraid to access them?

Take time to write down answers to these questions in a journal, and don't stop there! Below your answer, write any thoughts that come to your mind (no right or wrong) related to the question. For example, reflect on a specific memory or thought you have about a difficult or chaotic friendship. Make a list of feelings that come to mind as well.

SELF-CARE SYSTEMS

Friends, groups, and resources were the primary components of your social system. As you may be realizing, these connect directly with our next system: the self-care system. How you care for yourself is another key factor in managing (or not managing) life chaos.

Those who struggle with an out of control life tend to lack a daily routine. Maria, for example, is a 40-year-old single woman. She has a job in retail and her shifts vary from day to day and week to week. She goes to bed at different times every night and gets up at different times each morning. She hates grocery shopping so she either grabs something quick from the food court at the mall where she works or she just doesn't bother eating. She loves clothes and is meticulous about her appearance, but she often runs late because it takes her two hours to get ready to go out. Maria wouldn't call herself an alcoholic, but she does like to go out with co-workers and when she does she doesn't hold back. She recently began to experience some abdominal pain, but she hasn't had a chance to go to the doctor and she really doesn't want to go anyway.

If Maria sounds like a version of you, then you have some problems with your self-care system (and in her story you can see the overlap into her social system as well). She is not taking care of her body in any way, she has no structure to her daily life, and she is unlikely to move forward or even try to set life goals. One day bleeds into the next and years go by without any personal growth.

Every person is born with a basic set of needs, and these needs must be met for your

body and mind to function at their best. In general, an average adult needs the following self-care:
- 7-9 hours of sleep
- 3 consistent meals (or 5 smaller meals) at about the same time each day and comprised of healthy foods
- 3-5 periods of moderate exercise per week
- Connection with people daily
- Engagement in hobbies or pleasurable activities that do not harm you
- Yearly well-visits at the doctor and visits for unusual symptoms
- Medications (if needed) taken at the same time as prescribed daily
- General personal hygiene including clean clothes, showers, dental care, and hair care

Take a moment to re-read that list and think about your daily routine. Put a star next to the items that you have been neglecting.

One problem that can lead to a breakdown in the self-care system is a lack of self-awareness. In our example, Maria is not intentionally choosing to avoid self-care. In fact, she is strong in the area of personal hygiene and she spends hours maintaining this area. But she is not taking time to ask herself, "How am I feeling? What else do I need?" Instead, she assumes that she CANNOT take care of her sleep needs because of her job. She avoids a challenging situation (grocery shopping as a single person) and therefore neglects her eating habits.

The fact that you are reading this book puts you a step ahead of Maria. You are already trying to begin to increase your self-awareness by trying to evaluate the cause of your life chaos. Good for you! Now continue on your journey of self-awareness by asking yourself the following questions:

- How much sleep do I get each night?
- Do I have a consistent bedtime, waking time, and mealtimes?
- How much did I exercise last week?
- When I am in a bad mood, can I usually point to a reason or am I clueless as to why I am feeling the way I am?
- Do I have hobbies I enjoy? When was the last time I participated in these hobbies?
- Do I take time to do my hair, clean my clothes, or care for my physical appearance?
- What are some of the reasons (or excuses) I use to not take care of myself?

Some who struggle with a lack of self-care do not view themselves as worth taking care of. Others were not cared for as children so they do not know how to take care of themselves now. Still others feel "selfish" getting their own needs met and instead constantly meet the needs of others while neglecting themselves.

If any of these root issues resonate with you, take time to journal your thoughts before moving on. It may also be helpful to make a chart listing your daily needs in order to track your self-care.

VALUE SYSTEMS

Your value system is made up of several parts and is reflected in all the other systems we have discussed. To start with, the culture into which you were born shapes some of your values. A simple interview with an American contrasted with an interview with a Chinese person, for example, will demonstrate a wide difference in cultural values.

Some societies (tending to be known as "Western" cultures) value independence, creativity, challenging authority, and increasing your own financial advantage. Other societies (particularly "Eastern" cultures) place high values on community, cooperation, accepting your place in society, and financially supporting your parents. Sadly, Americans are often less aware of their own culture than many other parts of the world. Our "melting pot" can seem like a thick pea soup sometimes.

Your religious upbringing has a lot to do with your values as well. Whether you were raised Muslim, Christian, Buddhist, in a cult, or in any other faith, these experiences shaped your thinking. Some continue to hold the beliefs with which they were raised. For others, their upbringing or religious experiences caused them to question this faith and come to their own conclusions.

Everyone has values, whether they realize them or not. Everyone has a faith journey, whether they know they are on it or not. At some point, you have to ask the questions of faith: Where did we come from? What is truth? Is there a God? What is right and wrong? What happens when we die? These questions arise naturally because human beings are physical, emotional, and spiritual, with a body, mind, and soul.

In the introduction to this book, we talked about admitting the problem of a chaotic life. We had to acknowledge that we are unable to manage our lives ourselves. It is often at a point like this, where we come to the end of ourselves, that we connect with our value system strongly. We seek help, realize our own limitations, and desire to connect with something bigger than ourselves.

In addition to your culture and your faith, your view of yourself shapes your values. If you do not value yourself, you will not treat yourself or others with respect. You will not try to improve your life. You will accept chaos as the status quo for your life.

My pastor once said that you *do* what you believe. Anyone can *say* they believe in something, but your actions always speak louder than your words. To find out what you truly value right now, you have to take a look at your actions. What do your actions say about your culture, about your faith, or about your view of yourself?

Here are some questions that may help you as you reflect on your value system:
- In what culture was I raised? With what cultural groups do I identify?
- What are the top three values of my culture?
- What has my faith journey been like? Have I tried to find the truth?
- Are there things about my religious upbringing or culture that make me angry?
- How do I view myself? What do I see when I look at my reflection?
- What actions did I take today? How do these connect with my value system?

After you have written down some answers to these questions, take time to think about how you ideally want to act versus how you do act. Does your life reflect your values? Or do you say you value things that you do not actually prioritize? The discrepancy between your ideal life and your actual life will point to the root problems in your value system.

THE COMPLEX ECOSYSTEM OF YOU

All of these systems – family, social, self-care, and values – are interconnected and interdependent. How you were raised, who your friends are, where you spend your time, how you view yourself and take care of yourself, and what you believe about God and the world all together make up the complex ecosystem of *you*.

Hopefully in reading this chapter you have begun to increase your awareness of the problems in your systems. The very reason you see the same problematic patterns repeat over and over in your life is that the problem is bigger than any one incident in your life. Your decisions and choices tie back to your systems, and EVERY time you make a decision there is an impact on your life. Adding up a lot of individual decisions makes a larger impact. If you feel like your life is out of control and you have no idea where to start, there are problems in your systems.

In the next two chapters we will explore steps you can take to zero in on the roots of your life chaos and we will discuss strategies for changing your systems. Quick fixes or band-aid solutions will not work for systemic problems. You are not one New Year's resolution away from an orderly life. This kind of thinking only contributes to a lack of awareness of the depth of your life chaos.

As you read on, pay attention to your daily routines, your behavior patterns, and your thoughts. Keep a journal handy to write these down. Self-observation is the best way to gather information on ways to begin to change in a way that shifts your personal ecosystem.

3

FINDING THE ROOT

So far we have found some cracks in your various systems but that does not tell us what is the *cause* of the cracks. All we have identified so far are problem areas, but we still don't entirely know how those problems came to be in the first place.

The cause of the problem is what I will refer to as the "root issue." Simply identifying specific problems in your life does not mean that finding the root issue will be easy or obvious. Sometimes it requires further investigation into your life, and this process is sometimes difficult and painful.

I am reminded of a chilly fall morning when my husband and I woke up and discovered that our heating system was not working. We went down to the basement and investigated, assuming that the pilot light had gone out. Much to our surprise, the pilot light was fine and the furnace appeared to be working properly. We went back upstairs, now thinking that perhaps the heat was working but was simply not turned up high enough. The thermostat appeared to be in working order and set properly. Later that afternoon, having still not found anything wrong but definitely sure that our cold house was indeed the result of a lack of heat, we discovered a small switch on the wall. Somehow that switch, which controls the electricity connected to the furnace, had been accidentally turned off. Prior to that day we had no idea what the switch was for and we had never paid much attention to it. Suddenly we realized that something we had been unaware of before controlled something very important for our home.

Problems of life chaos are a lot like that heating system. Something is wrong – in our case it was the lack of heat. Our first guesses as to the root issue (pilot light problems or issues with the thermostat) turned out to be incorrect. It was only after a lot of time and consulting with friends who had more experience with heating systems that we discovered the true root issue. And it turned out to be something we had been ignoring all along.

Think back to some of the things you identified as problems before you began reading this book. Perhaps it was as simple as, "My life feels out of control." After you read and thought through the specific areas of life management, you may have narrowed that statement down a bit: "I have difficulty managing my time and this makes my life feel out of control." As you moved on to understanding the systems of your life, you may have begun to connect some of the dots: "I place a high value on people rather than on time. Also, when I was growing up my family was very disorganized. These factors contribute to my difficulty with time management."

You're almost there! You've dug deeper and deeper but we still do not know *why* you value people above time and we have not explored your family dynamic enough to know *why* and *how* it impacted you. These are critical questions because it will get us to the root issue so that we can solve the problem with a real solution.

I believe that there are several main categories of root issues. Whatever problems you may have identified in your systems are likely to have gotten there because of at least one of the following root issues: *skill deficiency, unmet needs, past hurts, personality issues, and biological/emotional disorders.* Let's examine each of these root issues more closely.

SKILL DEFICIENCY

For some, the heart of their life chaos problems is simply a lack of skills. This lack of skills most often ties back to problems in the family system. If your parents did not model stable, organized behavior then you would have to acquire it elsewhere (in your social system) in order to have it. An orderly life does not happen by accident.

We will cover specific skills related to life management later on in the book, but before task, time, relationship, or money management comes emotional regulation. If you do not have basic coping skills, you will not be able to apply any of the other skill sets successfully.

So what are coping skills and why do we need them? Coping is the ability to handle the problems and stressors you face. It is the voice in your head that says, "You can do this" or "It's going to be okay." (Watch an episode of *Mister Rogers* and you'll understand coping skills in less than 30 minutes!)

Coping is also about mood and emotion regulation. Understanding that your feelings are temporary is important if you do not want to have an impulsive reaction to them. For some, their adult models reacted very strongly to temporary feelings and situations. If this was your example, as an adult you may find yourself doing the same thing. Your feelings become in control of your life because you have no power over them. As a result, you have chaos in your life.

UNMET NEEDS

This second root issue goes a little bit deeper into the core of your emotional life. As a child you were born with a specific set of needs: to be changed, fed, held, and loved to name a few. As you grew older you needed wisdom, guidance, and positive role models. Sadly, many do not get these critical developmental needs met.

There are a variety of reasons for your needs to have gone unmet. If you look at each of the systems we talked about in the last chapter (family, social, self-care, and values), you will notice that you have needs in each of these areas. If your family was consumed with problems or neglected you in some way, or if you did not have a good social environment at school, for example, your needs were not met.

The impact of unmet needs is that you will continue to try to get your needs met in other ways. The saying, "Looking for love in all the wrong places" exemplifies this idea. If you did not experience love from your family or peers, you will keep trying to find it elsewhere.

If you were not given room to express yourself or take care of yourself because of pressure put on you to step into an adult role too soon, you may get stuck developmentally. Some of your life chaos may feel a bit adolescent. That's because it is teenager behavior!

When you identify unmet needs as a root issue, it is important to identify the age you were when your needs stopped being met. Often this reflects how "old" you are emotionally. If you were neglected as a toddler, you may find that you have two-year-old-sized temper tantrums. If your needs went unmet as a teen, you are likely to find that you respond to life much like a teenager would – impulsively. Try to connect your adult self with this younger version of you and offer yourself the love and wisdom that the younger you did not receive. (We will discuss this concept called "self-reparenting" in greater detail in the next chapter.)

Past Hurts

For some, the root issue goes far beyond needs going unmet. Abuse (verbal, emotional, physical and/or sexual) as well as general cruelty by family or friends can leave wounds that run very deep. Sometimes the pain from these past hurts can spill out into the rest of your life. You are most likely unaware of the connection between your past and your behavior now. You just know you have a short fuse, or you feel angry at the world. It may not be constant, but it can be often enough to disrupt your life and contribute to chaos.

Those with past hurts may find that their relationships are the most chaotic area of their lives. Sometimes this is because they are attracted to others who are again abusive to them. Sometimes they experience chaotic relationships because they themselves invite frequent conflict as they act their anger out onto others.

If you find yourself falling into this category, mindfulness is an important skill to practice. Mindfulness is simply the habit of being aware of your present surroundings and experiences. This can help you begin to separate your past from your present instead of allowing your past to spill into the present and disrupt it. (Keep an eye out for more detailed insights on mindfulness in the coming chapters.)

Personality Issues

Your personality is a complex and indescribable wonder. You are made up of unique preferences, desires, and abilities. But have you ever felt like you just got in your own way sometimes? The root of your life chaos may be quite ingrained into your view of yourself.

If you have been in counseling or have been around the mental health field, you may have heard of something called a "personality disorder." These are simply categories of symptoms that affect multiple areas of your life, specifically in the way you interact with others. Borderline, narcissistic, and antisocial personality disorders are just some of the specific disorders listed.

Personality disorders as well as general personality issues that do not fully meet the criteria of "disorder" are usually formed from maladaptive coping. Sometimes, but certainly not always, children who are abused find ways of coping with their situation that end up becoming problematic in their adulthoods. For example, what was once a healthy distrust of dangerous people in childhood becomes in adulthood an inability to trust others even when they are safe.

This root issue can be difficult to overcome, but healing is always possible. In part it is difficult because it is usually combined with at least one of the other root issues. If you find that you have disrupted relationships at work, at home, and in other settings you may need to work with a counselor to explore all of the root issues you are facing and find new ways of coping.

Biological/Emotional Disorders

A final root issue is found in biological and emotional disorders. You may have read through this chapter and thought, "I know I don't feel in control of my life, but I had a pretty good childhood, my needs were met, I was taught skills to manage life, and I wasn't abused. My relationships are pretty stable. But my feelings are definitely not in control." If you find yourself agreeing with this statement, you may be experiencing depression, mania, anxiety or another type of biological disorder of the brain.

Contrary to what you may want to believe, we do not have complete control over our emotions. We may be able to develop self-control over our actions and even our thoughts, but our feelings and thinking can be very difficult to control.

Sometimes we can point to a particular stressor that "set off" feelings that led to a deep depression or a bout of anxiety. However, mood or psychotic disorders can occur with no specific trauma or trigger. In addition, Attention Deficit and Hyperactivity Disorder (ADHD) begins in childhood and can carry chaos with it into adulthood. While we are only just beginning to understand disorders of the brain, we do have some basic knowledge that brain chemistry and functioning can wreak havoc on your emotional life.

If you have not been to a counselor or psychiatrist but you think you have some symptoms of a mental disorder, you should seek help. You should also have your primary care doctor rule out other conditions such as thyroid imbalance or even Lyme Disease that can have mood-affecting symptoms. Having suicidal thoughts or wishes for death is not normal, and if you feel suicidal you should immediately seek help at an emergency room.

Exercise, healthy eating, therapy, and medication can all be useful in getting a mood or psychiatric disorder under control. A team of providers, including doctors and counselors, can help you set up and maintain these routines.

A Final Note on Root Issues

Interwoven throughout all these root issues is your spiritual life. I have chosen not to make "spiritual issues" its own category because your relationship with God flows through every area of your life.

Imagine a large garden bed with many plants growing. Each plant has a root system, and often these root systems become intertwined. Underneath and surrounding all of these roots is the water in the ground. If a plant is doing poorly, the roots desperately need water to flow through them.

Your relationship with God can deeply nourish and heal your root system. Like a refreshing drink, connection with God will restore you. Disconnection from God, whether because of a sin issue in your life or from a lack of knowing God at all, will make any effort at healing temporary and incomplete.

As you work through the root issues that have come up for you in this chapter, pause to re-read the introduction to this book. Admit the root issues and surrender them to God. Seek the truth and seek relationship with God. It is only then that you can truly move on to our next chapter: making changes.

4

MAKING CHANGES

We have not taken all this time to get to the root issue only to stop there and say, "Great! Now I understand why I act the way I do." Insight is important, but it is how you apply that insight that makes all the difference. The entire point of going on this journey is to *change* your life, not make way for excuses as to why you are the way you are.

One reason that people often stop at gaining insight and understanding is that change is hard. Often therapists make this same mistake with their clients – they work their way all the way to the root issue, develop tons of insight, and then leave the behaviors right where they started. Why? Because real and lasting change is hard.

In the late '70s and early '80s, James Prochaska and his colleagues began to develop a theory about change. They began their study with people trying to quit smoking, but since the original studies many have applied their work to

a variety of other problems. They developed the concept of "stages of change" and identified the following stages in the process of change:
- *Pre-contemplation:* There is no awareness of a need for change.
- *Contemplation:* There is early awareness of a possible need for change but there is an internal conflict about whether or not to go through with change.
- *Preparation/Determination:* There is clear thinking about getting ready to change and a plan for change begins to form.
- *Action:* There are direct steps taken to begin the process of change.
- *Maintenance:* The change has been made and needs to be maintained.[6]

Notice that three out of these five stages of change do not involve any actual change in behavior at all! Change is not instant, it takes awareness, determination, planning, and persistence. You are very likely to experience significant emotions fighting AGAINST change. Even when your behavior is unhealthy or disruptive to your life, the fact that you know what to expect is a big motivator in keeping

---

[6] Prochaska, J. O., & DiClemente, C. C. (1983). Stages and processes of self-change of smoking: Toward an integrative model of change. *Journal of Consulting and Clinical Psychology*, 51(3), 390-395. Retrieved from http://www.samhsa.gov/co-occurring/topics/training/change.aspx

things the way they are. Fear of the unknown creeps onto the doorstep of change.

Another factor to consider as you seek to change is your "locus of control." This term was developed in the late 1960's by Julian Rotter, who conducted research on how your views about yourself and the world impact your ability to change. If you have an *external* locus of control, you believe that your life is mostly controlled by factors outside your control. If you have an *internal* locus of control you believe that your actions play a big role in the direction of your life.[7]

Stop and think about this for a moment. Do you believe that you can set a goal and accomplish it? Or do you believe that most good things happen by fate or by accident? Framing it in a more God-focused way, do you believe that God calls you to take action to make things happen in your life, or do you believe God will work it all out and you just need to sit back until He brings change about?

How you answer these questions makes a big impact on how you proceed next. In his writing on the topic, Herbert Lefcourt noted that people's views of their own ability to affect change in their lives is "seen to be of critical

---

[7] "Locus of Control: Are You In Charge of Your Destiny?" *Mind Tools*. Web. 12/29/2013.
If your are interested in assessing your locus of control, take this test on the Mind Tools website:
http://www.mindtools.com/pages/article/newCDV_90.htm

importance to the way in which they cope with stress and engage in challenges."[8] In other words, if you believe you can do something to change your life, you will be able to rise to the challenge.

But wait a minute... didn't we start this book declaring our powerlessness to manage life on our own? Doesn't this mean that I am unable to change my circumstances? No. When we place our lives underneath God's authority and surrender to Him, He leads us into better actions and thoughts. But we need to take action – after all, "following" implies action on our part. So in this process of change, let God lead you, but do not confuse this with doing nothing until God fixes it all for you.

Now that we've done a little exploring on the concept of change itself, let's go back to the root issues we identified in the last chapter and discuss steps you can take to begin the process of change. As we walk through each root issue, I want you to be asking yourself, "What stage of change am I in right now? Do I believe I am able to affect change in this area or does my gut tell me there's really nothing I can do to change this?" Feel free to flip back a few pages to the list of the stages of change as you evaluate yourself.

---

[8] Lefcourt, Herbert M. (1982). *Locus of Control: Current Trends in Theory and Research.* Hillsboro, NJ: Lawrence Erlbaum Associates Inc. p. 2.

Making Changes in Skill Deficiency

For those who identified skill deficiency as the root issue of their life chaos: great news! You may be lacking skills right now, but there are thousands of resources out there for you on improving your life management and coping skills. Your brain was designed to learn, and it is never too late to add to your knowledge base. Gaining skills is about learning as well as practicing, but over time you will find it possible to improve your skills.

The first step for you is to identify which specific skills you feel you lack. Do you have trouble coping with stress and this leads to chaos in your life as things spiral out of control? Do you lack specific relationship skills, such as communicating yourself or setting limits with others? Do you need to master specific time, task, or money management skills?

Once you know the specific skill set you need to gain, you then need to ask yourself, "Where and how will I learn this skill?" If you already have a counselor, then this is a great place to start. Ask your therapist for specific books or resources that might help you in your specific situation. If you do not have a counselor, I would recommend browsing the "Self-Help" section of your local bookstore. Many of these books will not be written from a Christian perspective, but if you can read with a critical mind and take the good from it, I believe many of these books can be useful.

Specifically you may want to do an internet search or a book search for "DBT skills." (This stands for Dialectical Behavioral Therapy and includes concepts such as mindfulness and emotion regulation.) Again be aware of the spiritual overtones in these concepts and evaluate from a Christian perspective how to best use these skills as they will help with coping and stress management.

You can also do a search for a specific skill, such as "task management" and browse the resources that pop up. In addition, chapters 6-10 of this book include a resources section at the end of each chapter that can give you specific titles as a starting point.

You should consider asking a friend, mentor, or counselor to read a book with you so that you may discuss it. If a specific book offers a companion workbook, I would encourage you to use it as well and do all the writing assignments given. Adding to your skills is not a speed-read. Take your time, talk it over with someone you trust, and find ways to apply what you learn in your daily life. Practice makes perfect!

MAKING CHANGES IN UNMET NEEDS

In the last chapter on root issues, I briefly mentioned the idea that when you have had unmet needs you need to begin to meet some of those needs that were neglected. The term "reparenting" has been used in a variety of ways in the field of psychology and many of the techniques have been controversial. I have personally found value in one modified form of this concept: *self-reparenting*.[9]

In self-reparenting, first developed by Muriel James, you first acknowledge the two parts of yourself that coexist. First, there is the adult you that lives and functions in very adult ways. There is strength in your adult self. Then there is also the part of you that did not properly develop because your developmental needs were not met. In the previous chapter I suggested that you pinpoint the age you were when your needs began to go unmet. This age helps identify the other part of yourself – the child inside you whose behavior is largely contributing to your life chaos.

Once you have more clearly understood these two parts of yourself – the adult and the child – you can begin to use the adult to meet the child's needs. Just as you would treat a child, your adult-self interacts with your child-self. You can give yourself love, encourage yourself in truth and wisdom, and also set limits on your child-self. This may sound like a strange concept at first, but I have seen it work with many of my clients.

The key here is that your adult-self can become the parent you never had. You can encourage yourself and nurture yourself, but you

---

[9] Gass, Michael A. *Rebuilding Therapy: Overcoming the Past For a More Effective Future.* (1997). Westport, CT: Praeger Publishers. p. 97.

can also reign yourself in. As you observe yourself, you will likely start to notice that your disruptive behaviors belong to the child-self.

You can set limits on these behaviors as you would with a child. I once had a client who set a limit on his child-self by not allowing the child-self to use the phone. When he noticed that he was reacting like a child (which took many months of self-observation to identify specifically), he would not allow himself to use the phone as it would only stir up conflict with his friends. Over time the child-self learned how to behave, and the child "grew up."

The ultimate goal of this type of self-reparenting is to develop your child-self until it is able to rejoin your adult-self. With this younger part of you now nurtured, you are whole again and can fully operate as an adult. When this happens you will find that the amount of chaos in your life decreases significantly.

When you have faced a root issue of unmet needs in your life, another important step is to begin to allow others to meet your needs. Your relationship with God as well as healthy relationships with people can meet needs that were neglected. You may find yourself resisting this help, as you have learned through experience that others can't be trusted to meet your needs. Working through those trust issues can be difficult, but finding one or two safe people in your life is a good start.

Depending on the level of work that needs to be done to change this root issue, you may want to consider seeking therapy if you have not already done so. A trained Christian therapist could be a safe person with whom you can develop trust and perhaps explore some of the self-reparenting techniques described. If you have had significant neglect or difficulty with trust, change may require additional help.

Making Changes in Past Hurts

When a person has experienced abuse or serious wounds from his or her past, it is very likely that professional counseling will be necessary. The nature of your experiences as well as your current symptoms will determine the extent of help needed. For this root issue I would suggest seeking counseling as a first step.

In the last chapter I also referenced mindfulness as a useful skill for those who have experienced past hurts. Securely knowing that the past is firmly in the past and that your present is now safe is critical to healing. Being aware of your present moment – the sounds, the smells, the feelings in your body – all of these observations can help you know you are no longer in the past.

As I mentioned earlier when we discussed skill deficiency, if you do an internet or book search for "mindfulness" you may find some non-Christian spiritual language. Other religions, such as Buddhism, use mindfulness as a spiritual technique to reach higher levels of spiritual enlightenment. I would encourage you to sift through these materials carefully and hold to the truth of the Bible as you explore them. I believe that Jesus was mindful – mindful of the moment, mindful of His mission, mindful of His Father, and mindful of His own personal needs and feelings. We are not seeking an alternate spiritual state. Rather, we are seeking to connect with the only moment we tangibly have – *right now*.

Forgiveness is also a key to healing from past hurts. You cannot move fully into the present until you have let go of the past. Forgiveness does not mean that those who hurt you are excused. Forgiveness does not mean that what happened was okay. Forgiveness does not make you forget. But it does allow you to clean your own heart of bitterness and anger that is harming you each and every day. If you are experiencing life chaos because the anger about your past is spilling out, the person or people who harmed you continue to have power over you. Forgiveness, because it is rooted in the very nature of God, cuts off the power of those who harmed you and frees you from your past.

Forgiveness is not a quick or instant experience. It is a process and there are many Christian resources available to you on the topic. If you search for "Christian forgiveness" on book retailer websites you will be able to browse a variety of helpful titles. Your church or another church in your area may also offer support groups for those healing from past hurts.

Making Changes in Personality Issues

Changes to personality issues can be difficult because this root issue can be more pervasive and may be entrenched in your understanding of yourself. For those dealing with personality issues that are negatively impacting a variety of areas of life, it can be extremely difficult to honestly evaluate oneself. You may have a lack of empathy and your mood may feel like a rollercoaster.

With the help of a counselor, the first step towards changing personality issues is to try to clearly identify your problem behaviors that are creating chaos in your life. You may find this difficult as you may tend to blame others for your life chaos. You may also push others away in order to avoid them rejecting you, making it difficult to be open to feedback from others. A counselor can help walk you through this process if you allow him or her in. (You may want to reject your counselor at some point, but try to hang in there for the sake of progress!)

After you have a specific list of consistent negative behaviors, consider how you have become the way you are now. I mentioned in the last chapter that this root issue is usually tied to at least one other root issue, so it may be that you have developed certain habits and traits as a result of trying to cope with unmet needs, past hurts, and/or skill deficiencies.

If this description of personality issues sounds like you, carefully read all of the other sections in this chapter about making changes.

You will need to combine the strategies because your root issues overlap. As I mentioned, therapy will be critical to change, and DBT skills have been used widely as an effective treatment for those with personality disorders.

The most important step you will need to take is to set aside your understanding of you. Most likely, your identity is in a fairly fragile state and you cling to it fiercely because it may feel like the only thing you know is certain in life. Your behavior in relationships may make you feel in control and safe. With the help of a professional Christian counselor, it is possible to begin to redefine your understanding of you, the world, and others. Be sure to read on to the next section of this chapter as well as it will also have tips for those dealing with biological/emotional disorders that may apply to your situation.

MAKING CHANGES IN BIOLOGICAL/EMOTIONAL DISORDERS

For those facing a biological/emotional disorder – such as depression, Bipolar Disorder, ADHD, anxiety, or a psychotic disorder – many of the ideas for change that have been mentioned so far will be of limited value. While behavioral changes are important, they are sometimes very difficult if not impossible when there are biological issues going untreated.

Your brain is a part of your body. Sadly, in some Christian circles, this truth is sometimes forgotten and emotional problems are considered fully within one's control. Although we do not yet have biological tests to precisely measure brain chemistry and functioning, the effective use of medications and the research that has been done to categorize symptoms is a start. Counseling and medication are an essential combination for those facing a disorder of the brain.

In addition to counseling and medication, regimented self-care is of the utmost importance. Daily routines, including adequate sleep, healthy food, and exercise can help take your out-of-control feelings and bring them into order. These habits will not come easily or naturally. You will have to fight yourself daily to stick to your routines even when your mood does not agree. Exercise in particular has been shown in a large number of studies to increase positive brain chemistry and boost mood.

You may want to go back to the section in chapter 2 about self-care systems. There you will be reminded of questions to ask yourself when developing a plan for self-care.

FINAL THOUGHTS ON CHANGE

Change is hard. When you look at the problems of your life, it often feels like an overwhelming mess over which you have no control. But big changes happen over time when you focus on making little changes. We devoted an entire chapter to systems for this very reason. A small change, like a tiny shift of climate either warmer or colder, can cause migration shifts or wipe out entire species. It doesn't happen instantly, but rather it occurs slowly over time. In the next chapter, we will focus on how to break down goals into measurable pieces to help you in this process.

As you move forward, keep this in mind: all of your systems will resist change. Your family and social systems will not want you to change (mainly because *they* also do not want to have to change). Your self-care system, even as chaotic and dysfunctional as it may be, is a set of habits that have gotten very comfortable. Your values system has been your framework for understanding the world, and changing this means you may have to admit you were... wrong! All of these changes sound unpleasant and scary. Yet the results of change over time will make you wonder what took you so long.

Do not attempt change alone. Real and lasting change takes time and hard work. Imagine training for a marathon with no one in your life encouraging you to keep at it. Most people would give up without support. If you don't have any supportive people in your life, you may want to consider counseling as well as finding a supportive church. Pastors, mentors, and counselors are great cheerleaders on this journey towards healing.

Now let's keep moving together and take a look at how to break down goals for change into small steps.

5

THE ROADMAP TO STABILITY

Congratulations! With all this talk of change, you would not have been the first to put the book down and say, "Maybe I'll keep reading that later..." But you've pressed through and here we are, ready to grab life by the horns and conquer your life chaos once and for all.

Now that we've zeroed in on the specific root issues in your life and we've talked about some ideas for moving forward, we next have to ask the toughest question of all, "*How* do I actually go about changing?" After all, if you could easily change habits that were making a mess of your life, you probably would have done it by now. You now know *what* to change, but the *how* is another matter entirely.

When you go on a journey, a map is helpful as you chart your course. A map offers direction and helps you pinpoint where you may have gotten off track. So let's map out some strategies for how to change in ways that are effective and lasting.

SET A MEASURABLE END GOAL

Simply saying, "I need to change the root issue of unmet needs in my life" isn't enough to actually move forward. Even saying, "I need to find ways to get my needs met" is not enough. When you want to make changes in your life, getting specific and measurable is key. This is a skill that may take some practice, particularly when you are a person that has struggled with chaos in your life. Rules, clear communication, and order may not be your thing (yet).

So take a moment and think about the root issue and ideas for change you have already figured out. (Hopefully you have had your journal or notebook handy as you have been reading – if not, don't hesitate to grab it now!) Once you are able to summarize the root issue in a sentence and have some ideas for change listed, you are ready to set a measurable goal.

Let's go back to our example, Maria, from chapter 2. (Refer back to the "Self-Care" section when we discussed the systems in your life.) Let's suppose that Maria has discovered that her root issue is unmet needs. She realized that she never learned to value herself because her parents didn't value her as a child. Both her parents worked all the time and really never had time for her. As an adult, she has taken on the same pattern – working above all else, neglecting her own needs and her own life.

Maria wants to change. Her first thought when setting a goal is, "I need to love myself more." That's a good start, but it is not measurable. How do you know if you love yourself *more* than you did before? Maria decides to get more specific: "I will eat healthy food to show that I care about myself." Again, this is a great idea but it not specific enough.

Finally, Maria lands on a goal that is specific and measurable: "I will go grocery shopping once a week on Tuesdays and will cook a recipe from *The Healthy Cookbook* six days per week."

Make A Realistic Plan

Now Maria is ready for the next question when setting goals: is my goal realistic? Maria set a specific and measurable goal, but was it realistic for her?

When thinking about making a goal realistic, it is important to think about your baseline. What is your behavior like right now? Let's look at Maria's baseline: right now she does not cook for herself at all. She doesn't remember the last time she went to a grocery store and she thinks she might know where her cookbook is but she may have to do some searching.

To go from her baseline of zero grocery shopping trips in recent memory and zero times she has cooked in the past month (or two!) all the way to shopping once a week and cooking six times per week is a bit of a stretch. It is unlikely that Maria will succeed in her goal because it is unrealistic. To fix this problem with her goal, she may consider changing the specifics – go grocery shopping twice in the next month, cook one healthy meal per week, etc.

In addition to being too far from her baseline, Maria's specific and measurable goal has two parts: go grocery shopping once per week on Tuesdays *and* cook from her healthy cookbook six times per week. Her goal also fails the test for being realistic because it is possible for her to succeed at one part (shopping) but fail at the other part (cooking). If this happens, will she have succeeded or failed at her goal?

Your realistic goal should be one small step from your baseline behavior and should only include one change. Once you master this small change, you can increase it. Maria may be able to *eventually* grocery shop once per week and cook six times per week, but she should work her way up to that level.

MAKE ONE CHANGE AT A TIME

As Maria has gotten going on all this goal setting, she decides she'd like to add a few more things to the list. She writes in her journal the following goals:
- Go to bed at 11:30pm every night. Wake up at 7:30am daily.
- Make at least 2 new friends and improve my relationship with God by going to church every Sunday.
- Talk to my boss about taking me off the schedule on Sunday mornings.
- Say no every time my co-workers ask me to go out for drinks.

- Set an alarm for one hour when I start getting ready to go out so that I will be on time.
- Call next Thursday to schedule an appointment with my doctor.

Maria looks over her list proudly. She is so excited she can't wait to get started. Specific goals? Check. Measurable? Check. Realistic? Mostly... She knows that regardless of her work schedule she is able to get to bed every night at 11:30 and wake up at 7:30. She is pretty good at making friends, so if her boss can keep her off the Sunday morning schedule she should be able to find some friends at the church she's been wanting to try. She's been getting tired of her co-workers so she thinks she can start saying no to them ("I just hope they don't start hating me...," she thinks.) She has an alarm she can set and she also knows she can make a phone call to the doctor.

Sounds like she's thought this all through, right? Just one problem: if you want real and lasting change you cannot make lots of changes at once. All of Maria's goals are reasonable and do-able. But she should not try them all this week. Remember when we talked about how hard change can be? Multiplying change is a whole lot harder!

Identifying specific ways you can change your life can be a scary but very exciting process. It is common to get carried away and gain emotional momentum so that you make a lot of rapid changes that all last for a very short time. I hope that anyone reading this book can have a life that is changed for the better, not an enthusiastic week.

So take a deep breath. Slow yourself down. Real and lasting change takes time. Look at your list and prioritize. What change is the easiest to make? Try starting with that one. When you've mastered that, move on to the next on your list.

This slow-and-steady approach can be discouraging as you may feel that the chaos in your life isn't going away fast enough. If Maria starts by simply going to the grocery store twice in a month or cooking once per week, most of her life chaos will still be there. She may succeed at her goal but at the same time not really see the point if it's not going to make a major dent in her out-of-control life.

One of the reasons change is so hard is because it is so slow. Maria can feel proud of herself for making a step towards life change. She can focus in on that one goal for a time, and after a month or so of success she can add another change. Over time, her life will be dramatically different even though she never felt like she made a dramatic change.

If you can embrace this concept you will be totally set free in your process of change. Looking at the whole, overwhelming picture of your messy life is where you started on this journey. Now that you know you are free to just do one small piece at a time, there is so much hope for the life you've been wanting.

When we recognize our own limitations and work within these (focusing on one small piece at a time), we accept a proper view of ourselves. This view also allows us to have a proper view of God and His role in the process of change. We can trust Him to bring about change in our hearts and minds as we are diligent to do the one part we can handle for today.

Expect Small Failures

Setting specific, measurable, and realistic goals does not guarantee success. Your plan will not go perfectly. In fact, it is common when you take steps forward in life to run into a higher level of chaos before things settle down. If you plan for small failures you will be able to overcome them more easily.

Maria has decided to go grocery shopping twice this month. She wants to buy healthy foods like fruits and vegetables, but she is going to buy mostly quick and easy items rather than do a lot of meal planning right away. The first week she did well, and the grocery store was not as intimidating as she expected it to be. She felt great and even ate a banana on the way home.

A few days later, Maria got a call from her boss. The assistant manager was quitting suddenly and Maria was needed for more shifts. "This could be my chance at a promotion and a raise," Maria thought. "It will only be for a couple of weeks and then things will settle down." Unfortunately, the extra work hours lasted for a month and Maria fell back into eating take-out.

Should Maria give up at this point? After all, she could not even meet her simple goal of going to the grocery store twice! Too often, this is as far as people get in the process of change. Life does not cooperate with your plans to live differently. Don't give up simply because you do not succeed on your first try.

We all have choices, and right now is a great time to reflect on your priorities in the coming months. For Maria, it would have been a big step for her to say no to her boss when he said she needed to come in for extra hours. (She didn't end up getting that promotion after all...) Maria may not have been ready to do something as drastic as putting limits on her work schedule, but if you learn from her experience you may be more prepared for your next tough decision.

Think about all the things that could go wrong as you begin to make life changes. Pause and write a list. You may not catch all the possibilities, and certainly not everything you think of will happen. But think in general about the patterns that you've started to notice. What happens to throw you off course? What are some of those holes in your life systems that may pop up during this change process?

Expect some of these patterns to disrupt your ability to perfectly accomplish your goals. Write down some options for responses you could have when faced with "failure." Remember to be encouraging – don't beat yourself up!

Here are some responses you could include on your list:
- I will not stop trying to succeed at my goal even if I have a bad day.
- Change happens slowly and I will not succeed perfectly or quickly.
- I would fail far more if I stopped trying to make life changes than if I simply was imperfect in my efforts.
- God offers grace to me and I will offer grace to myself as well.
- Failing to reach my goal gives me an opportunity to discover problematic patterns in my life systems.
- I can always re-evaluate my goals if I was not realistic at first.

Summing It All Up

Have I mentioned change is hard? You are a complex human being with complex relationships and systems in your life and you live in a complex physical and spiritual world. There is a lot you cannot control! This reality is what makes people stick to what they feel they CAN control – patterns of behavior they are used to – even if it disrupts their lives.

Focusing on one small goal at a time can give you a real sense of control. There are a lot of things in life that we try to control yet we have no actual control over them. When you view yourself as a limited human person, living under a loving and merciful God who desires more for your life, you begin to take control of the things you actually *can* control. You can gain control of yourself and your own behavior, one little step at a time. And you can leave the rest up to God.

So go ahead, take that step. It may not revolutionize your life tomorrow, but it is a step in the right direction. As you succeed at the first small step, you will gain momentum and you will feel better about yourself. That "locus of control" that we talked about in chapter 4 will begin to shift from external (everything around me determines my life) to internal (there are things I can do to make changes). A year from now, you may have taken ten or twelve small steps that add up to a pretty big difference. Just ask anyone who has saved up for a vacation with spare change!

6

TASK & TIME MANAGEMENT

Now that we've figured out how to begin the process of change, we're ready to dive into specific skills that will help you move forward in life management. We have identified the systems at work in your life, we have explored the root issues, and we made specific, measurable, and realistic goals. The rest of the book is designed to be a blueprint for a more orderly life. In each chapter I will describe four concrete skills you can practice in your daily life.

In chapter 1 we discussed various areas of life that require proper management. Because task and time management skills have a lot of overlap I have chosen to put them together into one chapter. Take a moment to go back to chapter 1 and re-read the stories Sheri and Bill in the task and time management sections.

Sheri, who has always struggled with task management, has identified root issues of skill deficiency and a biological/emotional disorder (ADHD). She has struggled since childhood with completing tasks and her parents never seemed to be able to help her find a way to manage life that worked for her. Her starting goal is to check the washing machine every evening right after dinner to make sure she has switched the load to the dryer. She is also considering talking to her doctor about medications that may help her focus.

Bill, our time management example, has figured out that his value system weighs heavily on people over tasks. His social system is very big, but his self-care system is underdeveloped. He now feels that his root issue may be personality. He's a dynamic, extroverted guy who loves attention but this gets in the way when he needs to get things done. When no one is paying attention to what he's doing and he's all alone, he just can't find the motivation to accomplish anything useful.

Sheri and Bill both need to develop their task and time management skills. The four skills we will highlight here will help them both improve their life stability.

DEVELOP A DAILY ROUTINE

A daily routine is simply a set combination of habits. Good habits do not develop on their own. I have never met anyone who accidentally got in shape or who inadvertently began following a budget. These types of life habits take time, investment, planning, and diligence. Bad habits, on the other hand, are quite easy to fall into and can be difficult to break.

Developing a daily routine will make changes to your self-care system, and these changes may impact your other systems as well. If, for example, you and your friends are used to hanging out every night until very late and you want to make a daily routine that includes getting to bed by 10:30pm, you will need to make changes in your social system. Your family system may be impacted if you want to have a daily exercise routine as your spouse and children may expect you to spend that time with the family. If you explain to your friends and family what your goals are and why you want to develop new habits, they might be more supportive to the changes you are making.

So just how do you go about developing a daily routine and what should be included? The list in the "Self-Care" section of chapter 2 gives you a start. A set bedtime and wake time, exercise, and healthy eating along with routines for getting things done at work and at home are important. When do you usually wake up? What do you do immediately upon waking up? What do you do before leaving the house? What do you do between leaving the house and getting to your final destination? How do you spend your day and your evening? What do you do right before bed? When do you go to bed?

All of these questions can help you examine your life now. If there is no *usually* in any of these areas then you need to start with one habit. Choose one of the items on the self-care list and start there. Do it every day in the same way at the same time. Once you have developed one habit, you can add another.

Most likely you already have at least one thing you do every day that is good for you. Brushing your teeth, for example, is a habit most people have in the morning and/or before bed. Sometimes it is helpful to pair a new habit with an already established one. For instance, you may develop a new Bible reading routine by deciding that you will put your Bible near your toothbrush and immediately after brushing your teeth you will read a verse or chapter. Once you have that down, you can add another habit to that routine.

If you start with one habit and continue to add to it one more habit at a time, you will develop a routine. This routine will begin to provide an anchor for your life, bringing order to the chaos.

Make a Priority List

What is most important to you? This is a critical question for anyone trying to improve task or time management. If you have no idea what task should come first or in what way you should spend your time, your life will be chaotic and haphazard.

List making is a key strategy for prioritizing. After you make your to-do list, you can rank tasks in order of importance and even write a specific date and time when you will do the task.

Make sure that your tasks are specific and can be done in one step. "Buy a new car" is too general for a list as it involves many different steps. First you may need to figure out how much money you have to buy the car. Then you may want to research different types of cars to narrow your options. Next you could look online at car listings and compare sales by owner versus a dealership. After this you will need to make a phone call, send an email, or go in person to see the car you want to buy. You may have to fill out paperwork, get inspections, and register the car. We just listed at least 8 different steps! Each one of them needs to be listed separately on your task list.

Our task management example, Sheri, struggles with symptoms of ADHD. She will need something outside of her own head to keep track of tasks. And she has to write tasks down in the same place in the same way every day.

If you do not already have an agenda book or planner, get one! You can use your phone calendar as well, which is helpful for some who need reminder alarms. In the last section of this chapter I will list specific resources for planners that can help with list making and task/time prioritization.

ACCEPT YOUR LIMITATIONS

I hate to be the one to break it to you, but you are a limited and finite human being. You cannot do it all. This truth can be a hard pill to swallow for people whose lives are busy and chaotic. It just feels so *possible* to do everything right now!

After you have accepted the fact that you need to set limits on your time and tasks, you will have to begin say "no" (cringe!). Yes, that's right... that N-O word that most two-year-olds could easily demonstrate for you is one of the hardest things you need to master.

If you have chaos in your life, I almost guarantee you have difficulty saying "no." You have to say "no" to others, and you have to say "no" to yourself. You will need to say, "No, self, I do not have time to do one more thing before I leave the house...." and "No, self, I cannot sit down on the couch again until I do the next task on my list."

You will have to say "no" to even good things, like volunteering for (yet another) church ministry or giving rides to anyone who ever asks you for one. We will talk more about this skill – boundary setting – in the next chapter when we cover relationship skills.

Find Your Motivation

Our time management example, Bill, has motivation problems. He does well when he is the center of attention, but he does not care much about tasks that won't get noticed. This is one way a "Why bother?" attitude can present itself.

There are many types of "Why bother?" attitudes that you can find among people who struggle with task and time management. Understanding the concept of your love language

– a concept developed by Gary Chapman[10] – can help you discover your "Why bother?" struggles.

In his book, Chapman describes five different ways people give and receive love: quality time, words of affirmation, physical touch, acts of service, and gift giving. In our example, Bill most likely thrives on quality time and words of affirmation. If he does not get these things, his tasks and time may feel wasted.

You may struggle with doing household tasks that will go unnoticed. Or you might some tasks to be boring and meaningless if it is only for yourself rather than for someone else. What makes you tick? What is your motivation to get things done, and when do you notice yourself saying, "Why bother?"

The amount of emotional space in your life affects your time and task management as well. You will not be motivated to do less-than-pleasant tasks if you are stressed out and burned out. When we get to a place where we have not had a habit of accepting our limitations, we become unmotivated to do even things we once enjoyed. If you feel drained from your life or sick of the chaos, you will find it difficult to motivate yourself to keep moving forward.

A period of time in which you feel like your life is getting worse instead of better is very un-motivating. You've gotten used to the idea

---

[10] Chapman, Gary. (2010). *The 5 Love Languages: The Secret to Love That Lasts*. Chicago: Northfield Publishing.

that your life is on a chaotic path and you've resigned yourself to the notion that there's really nothing you can do.

Remember when we talked about change? Your locus of control is external – you have no sense that you can influence events in your life. But now that you've done some digging and are hopefully seeing life in a new light, your motivation can come from a place of belief that God has given you the ability to move forward.

So pause right now, pull out that journal, and make a list. Start with this question: What are my reasons for changing my life? You might list your relationship with God, your kids, or simply a desire to feel better. Whatever your motivation, make sure you have it clearly defined because you are going to need it when you feel like giving up.

FURTHER RESOURCES

There are quite a lot of resources available to you if you are looking to go further in your task and time management skills. Personal planners are a good place to start. Franklin Covey is a leadership and management guru that has a variety of planners specifically designed to help you organize your life. If you have a smartphone, there is a free Franklin Covey Tasks app as well as additional apps for purchase.

Tasks and time management books are plentiful and each will appeal to a different audience. Depending on how your brain works,

you may find some of these to be helpful resources:
- *Time Warrior* by Steve Chandler (2011)
- *Time Management from the Inside Out* by Julie Morgenstern (2004)
- *Organize Your Mind, Organize Your Life* by Margaret Moore and Paul Hammerness (2011)
- *ADD-Friendly Ways to Organize Your Life* by Judith Kohlberg and Kathleen Nadeau (2002)

The above list of books is merely a starting point. Stroll down the business management or self-help sections of your local bookstore or search on an internet book retailer and you will find hundreds more. Any of the books I have listed (and any additional books you may find) should of course be read with a goal to take the good and leave what doesn't fit for you. No resource is perfect, but it may help you develop some new skills.

7

RELATIONSHIP MANAGEMENT

Relationships can be one of the hardest areas of life chaos to change. As I mentioned in chapter 2, relationship systems (including your family and social systems) are complex and have a life of their own. You are not entirely in control of these systems – they have at least one if not multiple other people contributing to them.

In his book, *The Tipping Point*,[11] Malcolm Gladwell talks about a phenomenon that can be seen in pop culture that I think also applies to relationships. He outlines a variety of examples, from footwear to crime rates, in which little change was evident until a specific moment – the tipping point – after which change skyrocketed. In relationship systems, change can be hard and you may not see a lot of progress until you find the right tipping point.

---

[11] Gladwell, Malcolm. (2002). *The Tipping Point: How Little Things Can Make A Big Difference.* New York: Back Bay Books.

So just what is a relationship tipping point? Think about relationships you have been in that have changed, either for better or for worse. Something has brought you closer together or driven you apart. Some tipping points are out of your control, such as tragic events like a death, house fire, or natural disaster. But you may be able to create other types of tipping points that can produce real change in your family and social systems.

Before we get into specifics, let me pause to warn you that I will be encouraging you to end some of your relationships. Sadly, we may have to tip your most chaotic relationships towards their undoing. These losses of relationship will be painful and difficult, but if you truly want freedom from chaos in your life you will need to surrender them.

If you are ready, let's explore some tipping points you can create in your relationships. These four skills will strengthen good relationships or end negative ones.

Trust

According to Erik Erikson's theory of human development, the very first stage everyone goes through is "trust versus mistrust."[12] Babies who are adequately nurtured learn that they can trust others and that the world is safe. Infants who do

---

[12] Erikson, Erik. (1982). *The Life Cycle Completed.* New York: W.W. Norton & Company, Inc.

not receive that care often distrust others and avoid intimacy.

Even if you were taken care of as a child, many later wounds in life can lead to mistrust of others. A friend's betrayal, an unrequited love, or an unexpected end of a relationship can all bring on defensiveness and walls that shut others out.

On the other extreme, some of us have almost no filters when it comes to trust. Those in this category tend to see everyone as worth trusting, which of course anyone at a used car dealership can tell you is not accurate!

Trust must be earned, and it is a tipping point for any relationship. Healthy relationships start slowly. If you meet someone, you do not necessarily trust them with the most private details of your life right away. You may trust them enough to tell them your first name, the town you are from, or your favorite kind of pizza. But hopefully you would not hand over your bank account number to them on the first handshake.

Flip back to chapter 1 and look for the section on relationships. Our example, Jocelyn, had trust problems. Although some trust problems involve trusting no one, for Jocelyn it is the opposite. After only a two week friendship, she invites a "friend" to come live in her house. She trusts that they will respect her belongings, not let in strangers, not bring drugs or alcohol into the house, and leave after a few days. Yet there is no way Jocelyn has enough information to know for sure that her new friend is *worth* trusting in any of these areas.

The key to the trust tipping point in a relationship is to determine which people in your life are worth trusting. Some of these people will be people that you'd like a relationship with – those whom you have known for a while but have been too afraid to let in. Others on your list will be people who have hurt you in some way or added to the chaos in your life.

Pause now and make a list with two columns: people to trust and people not to trust. Place everyone you can think of – friends, family, co-workers, acquaintances – in one of those two categories.

Now here's the tipping point: take those in the "not to trust" column and begin to take steps away from the relationship. Consider deleting their phone numbers from your phone. Next time they ask you to spend time with them, say you'd rather not. Stop initiating contact or spending time together. (We'll talk more about setting boundaries in the next section to give you more ideas).

At the same time, tip your positive relationships into greater intimacy and trust. If there is someone you have wanted to open up to but have been afraid of being judged or rejected, take a step of faith. Call up that person you've said no to before and see if he or she is available for coffee. The more you fill your schedule up with positive people, the less time you will have to give to those who are not worth trusting.

Honesty is the key here – you increase trust by sharing honestly over time. Don't rush it – instead slowly step into vulnerability with those who have demonstrated they deserve your trust. Having 2-3 close friends with whom you can share your deepest feelings safely is plenty, and everyone else can remain a casual friend or acquaintance.

Boundaries

Developing trusting friendships and ridding your life of negative friends and family members brings us right to our next relationship skill: boundaries. One of the best books I have ever read on relationships has that simple title – *Boundaries*.[13] In their book, Henry Cloud and John Townsend present a detailed Christian argument for why boundaries matter and how to implement them in your life. If relationships is an area of life chaos for you, read their book (right after you finish this one!).

Boundaries are simply barriers you put up that define "you" and "not you." Just as a map has clear lines where one country ends and another

---

[13] Cloud, Henry and Townsend, John. (1992). *Boundaries: When to Say Yes, How to Say No to Take Control of Your Life*. Grand Rapids, MI: Zondervan. They have added books to this series as well, so look for other *Boundaries* books by these authors specific to dating and marriage.

begins, so too your life needs to be carefully drawn up with boundary markers. There are a few spots around the globe where the boundary lines are not clear, and certainly chaos is the result. Wars continue to be fought when boundary lines are in question. Redefining boundaries in your relationships may feel a bit like a war, and taking this step will certainly produce a tipping point in your relationships.

So what exactly are boundaries and how do you set them in your life? Some examples of boundaries include how frequently you see or talk to someone, how much personal information you share, how much you give or take from another person, and the general rules that you allow your relationships to follow.

I have a boundary with my children defining the rules for how they are allowed to talk to me. They do not have to always agree with me, but they do need to speak calmly and without blaming or attacking me. My side of that boundary line is that I carefully listen to them and make sure they know they have been heard. There is mutual respect given even though they know that I have the final say.

Setting boundaries can be difficult if your root issue is either unmet needs or past hurts. This difficulty is due to the fact that you did not have models of good boundaries from the adults in your life and also because you had your boundaries violated over and over again. If you have been harmed in this way you are likely to have one of two reactions: put up a brick wall so that no one can have a relationship with you or let in everyone with absolutely no boundaries to protect yourself.

Let's pause again and think about your relationships. Pull out that list you made of people to trust and people not to trust. For those who have hurt you who no longer deserve your trust, what kind of boundaries do you need with them? For some, it may be to cut them out of your life completely. In this case the boundary would be, "I will not talk to or see this person again," or "This person can no longer be allowed to live with me." For others, it may be less drastic, such as "I will talk to my mother once per week instead of every day," or "I will not visit my hometown more than once per year." For less intimate relationships, you may decide on a boundary like this one: "I will not give my phone number to people I have just met."

Often once you set a boundary you may find that you have a difficult time keeping it in place. After all, if following through with boundaries were easy, you would have already done it! It is easy to back down in the face of family and social systems that are resistant to change. Accountability is essential here – find a safe person like a mentor, counselor, or pastor to hold you accountable on the boundaries you set.

Boundaries are a tipping point in the relationship, moving you out of relationship with people you should not trust. But for those people you *can* trust, you will still need boundaries. Healthy friendships develop slowly, and if you are not used to boundaries in a relationship you are likely to violate a healthy person's boundaries without meaning to. Set limits on yourself, calling a new friend no more than once per week and respecting them if they set boundaries with you.

COMMUNICATION

Setting boundaries requires an additional set of skills: communication. You can't set healthy boundaries without communicating them clearly. When people try to set boundaries without communication, it usually backfires. A possible exception would be someone with whom you are trying to completely cut off contact. You can block them on your phone, Facebook, etc. without directly telling them you plan to do so. Even this, however, will sometimes backfire as the person finds ways around blocks to find out why you have suddenly stopped communicating. In general, any person with whom you want to maintain a relationship ought to know clearly what you are thinking and feeling.

Communication in relationships goes beyond just boundary setting. Expressing your thoughts, feelings, and needs is also essential for any healthy relationship. Intimacy grows as people share themselves with one another – it is the very essence of knowing and being known. Even God chose to use communication in order to make Himself known, bringing forth His very word in the Bible.

Self-expression is often very difficult, especially if you have been hurt or ignored in the past. Have you ever felt like talking to a brick wall would be more effective than talking to your spouse, friend, or family member? At least a brick wall doesn't interrupt!

The other communication skill you will need to focus on is listening. We sometimes forget this very important skill when we think about communication, but without it we are right back to the brick wall scenario. Listening involves active work as you process what someone is saying and reflect it back to them.

Improving communication in a relationship requires at least two people who are both interested in changing the system. This is because communication is a two-way street. If someone with whom you are in a relationship is not interested in working on improved communication skills, put them on the "Don't Trust" list! Use your boundary setting skills to distance yourself from them, because there is little chance for improvement. (In the case of a marital issue, if both parties are willing to go to counseling don't give up! Even if you are not on the same page about improving the communication at first, there is hope for reconciliation.)

If you have identified at least one person who is willing to work on communication skills with you, set up specific times – maybe once per week – to intentionally practice. One exercise that may be helpful is taking turns expressing one thought or feeling. After a brief thought is expressed, the listener repeats back to the speaker what he heard. If the listener does not get it right, the speaker can restate their thought to be more clear. After each expressed and understood thought, switch roles and repeat the exercise.

Effective communication involves rules, as we discussed in chapter 2 in our overview of family and social systems. Your communication rules can include some of the following:

- Everyone is given respect by getting a chance to speak without interruption.
- We use "I feel" statements ("I feel sad when you are on your phone the whole time we go out") instead of blaming or attacking statements ("You are such a jerk. You love that phone more than you love me!")
- There is room for healthy conflict and disagreement because we know we are committed to loving each other. We verbally remind each other of this commitment during and after conflict ("We're all on the same team.")
- Threats of leaving the relationship are not allowed. Instead, boundaries are established and followed when needed.
- We will not intentionally push each other's buttons or try to verbally harm each other.
- We will take a break from arguing when someone says "Time out!" and we will set

a time to return to the conversation when we have cooled off.
- Each person will do what they say they will do to the best of his or her ability.

These communication rules are just a starting point. Add your own ideas as you think about the problem areas in your communication. Slowing down your communication and/or changing the rules for your family and social systems can be hard work. Don't give up! If you keep at it, you will hit that relationship tipping point when the rules will be second nature.

Conflict Resolution

Some of the communication skills we just listed directly relate to conflict resolution. And all of them aim at escalated conflict *prevention*. Not all conflict is bad; in fact, I believe that all healthy relationships have conflict from time to time. But *escalated* conflict is toxic in a relationship because it involves words and actions that can hurt long after the conflict is over.

The Bible has numerous references to the fact that God is slow to anger.[14] Let your mind sit on those words for a moment – *slow to anger*. Do those words describe you? If not, why do you

---

[14] See Exodus 34:6, Numbers 14:18, Nehemiah 9:17, Psalm 86:15, Psalm 103:8, Psalm 145:8, Joel 2:13, Jonah 4:2, Nahum 1:3 (New International Version).

think that is? Often when people are quick to become angry it is because they are carrying anger inside them wherever they go. They have chaotic relationships full of conflict because they are just angry at the world. Angry at life. Maybe even angry at God.

Jocelyn, our case example in this chapter, struggles with this too. If you'll notice when she was introduced in chapter 1, she has ongoing conflict with her mother that repeatedly results in the two of them not speaking to each other. It is unlikely that these arguments are actually about the issue at hand. Repeating patterns of conflict such as Jocelyn's go far deeper. What is the one thing she feels her mother will never understand? In what ways have she and her mother hurt each other?

Perhaps you started thinking about your relationships when we explored the root issue in chapter 3. Those root issues you identified may give you insight into your conflict. What is the brokenness you carry into every argument? What are some ways you can find healing in those areas of pain?

Finding the heart issue underlying your conflict will move you towards that tipping point when you can release it and feel freedom. Whatever that deepest root is, you can find comfort and healing by allowing Jesus in. Go back to chapter 4 in our section on making changes to past hurts to re-read about the role of forgiveness in the healing process as well.

FURTHER RESOURCES

Earlier in this chapter I mentioned the book *Boundaries* by Cloud and Townsend. Here are some other books on relationships that you may find helpful:
- *Beyond Boundaries: Learning to Trust Again in Relationships* by John Townsend (2011)
- *The Dance of Anger* by Harriet Lerner (2005)
- *People Skills: How to Assert Yourself, Listen to Others, and Resolve Conflicts* by Robert Bolton (1986)
- *Why Don't We Listen Better? Communicating & Connecting in Relationships* by James Petersen (2007)
- There are many other titles by Henry Cloud and/or John Townsend – look for them all!

Relationship skills take time to develop. Practice in safe places with safe people. Read these and other resources slowly with a pen and notebook by your side to write your thoughts. Deepening your relationships is as much about self-reflection as it is about skill development. Until you understand why you keep going back to unhealthy relationships, you will continue to repeat the same chaotic patterns.

8

MONEY MANAGEMENT

When you think of money management, you may think of investing, stock markets, and 401(k)'s. But if your life has been in financial chaos, you have to start a lot closer to the basics. The most basic and fundamental financial principle lies deep within you: your view of money.

Some people view money as a tool. Others view it as a necessary evil. Still others view it as an idol (though they may not come right out and say it!). Is money something you use strategically to move forward in life? Is money something you hate thinking about? Or is the pursuit of money something that is in the driver's seat of your life?

When I was growing up, my parents were the financial counselors for our church. I remember countless nights hovering around the dining room entry, watching my parents talk with people who were in dire straits. Their lives were completely unmanageable because their financial lives were out of control. I learned very early the real sense of desperation you feel when you are trapped by money.

I have had a budget since I got my first allowance of $1 per week. (Don't even think of telling me that you don't make enough money to have a budget!) Each week I would put 10 cents towards my tithe for the church, 10 cents for fish food, 20 cents for savings, and 60 cents for free spending. As I got older, my allowance grew and my budget expanded. I had to keep careful track in a ledger and if there was a calculation error my mom and I would sift through until the numbers added up.

One day when my parents were teaching a Sunday school class on budgeting, I came into the classroom before they had finished up. My parents put me in the role of teacher (I was probably 10 or less) and began to ask me some questions to answer for the class of adults. They said, "Kristen, if you have 10 cents in your free spending category and 20 cents in your fish food category and you want to buy gum for 25 cents, can you buy it?" Appalled by the thought of exceeding my budget category I said, "No way! I only have 10 cents to spend on the gum!" The adults laughed at the simplicity of it all, and probably felt slightly embarrassed at being out-budgeted by a 10-year-old.

The Bible does not say that money is the root of all evil. It does say that the *love of money* is the root of "all kinds of evil," meaning there are many ways in which you can do things you never thought you would do if money is an idol in your heart.[15] I do not believe Judas Iscariot, for example, intended from the start to betray Jesus. But as the treasurer for the disciples, he took a little off the top here and a bit in his pocket there and before he knew it money was in control of his decision making.

Is that you today? Are you finding yourself doing things you never thought you'd do for the sake of money? Has money trapped you so completely that you are no longer free to live the way you want to live? There is hope and there are ways out of the mess. Let's take a look now at some ways you can start to turn things around.

Examine Your Heart

There are deeper issues ruling your financial chaos besides the actual numbers. One central heart issue concerning money is a lack of contentment. I have heard countless people say, "I wouldn't have problems with money if I only had more of it." Think again! If you have chaos in your financial life, the discontentment will only grow as you get more money. There will always be someone with more than you.

Flip back to chapter 1 and take a moment to re-read Sam's story in the section on money management. He has lived with a problem with his values system – money is too high on the list.

---

[15] 1 Timothy 6:10. See the New Living Translation or New International Version.

At the core (though he'd never admit it), Sam believes that having more money and more stuff will make him happier. Given the high percentages of wealthy celebrities who are living drug-addicted lives and/or commit suicide, I think it's safe to say money is not the key to happiness.

Fear is another common heart issue related to money. Fear of failure, fear of not having enough, fear of losing independence, fear of going without. Those with this heart issue tend to be the over-savers – people who might be called "stingy" or "tight-fisted." Sometimes this heart issue goes undetected because there is less direct financial chaos present, but there is chaos of the heart.

So why does Sam give in to discontentment and fear? One huge reason is that as an American he is surrounded by a culture that is designed to produce discontentment and fear in his life. Every commercial and billboard counts on him wanting more, needing more, never being satisfied until he has what they are selling. If we have opened our minds to what the world is selling, we will never have enough.

Another reason Sam believes that more money will solve his problems is a lack of emotional awareness. He knows he feels discontented or afraid, but he does not know the underlying reason. Because he just feels a feeling in his gut, he tries to fill that void and cover up that feeling with a quick fix. Yet the quick fixes Sam tries only make the problem worse as he becomes further and further dissatisfied. (And yes, even Christians with a relationship with Jesus can still have this feeling of a void since growing in spiritual and emotional health is a lifelong journey).

Exploring the systems and root issues we discussed in chapters 2 and 3 can help you move beyond Sam in your ability to understand the true nature of your problems. If Sam really took time to look at his value systems, he may find that what he *says* he believes and how he acts are actually very different.

Working through his root issues, Sam may come to discover that his needs weren't met adequately, or that he simply never had models to teach him money management skills. It is possible that Sam approaches his relationships in the same way that he approaches his own emotional life, using money to fix it. He may be a classic example of a father who has no idea how to relate to his children and instead tries to buy them gifts or "stuff" to win their approval.

Others, like the classic Ebeneezer Scrooge, may try to save or hoard money in an effort to feel a sense of security. Perhaps a sense of security and safety was an unmet need in childhood, or perhaps there is a spiritual issue for those who have not been able to surrender money to God or trust that He will provide for their needs.

Where do you think your heart issues lie? In what ways has money taken over your values system? Do you use money and shopping to cope? Do you feel in control of your spending or does it control you? What role does money play in your quest for satisfaction, or in your approach to relationships? Before moving on to the next sections that will offer practical money management skills, be sure you have begun the journey of healing your heart.

TRACK YOUR SPENDING

Once you have acknowledged and begun to address the heart issues related to money, you can take some practical steps to decrease financial chaos. The starting point is to track your spending. If you have no idea where your money is going, you will have no ability to control your financial life.

You can track your spending in a variety of ways. If you use mainly cash, get a receipt for everything you spend. If you use a debit card, print your monthly bank statements and review. If you primarily use credit cards, you should probably stop. Unless you are paying your full balance each month, you should not use a credit card.

Once you know what you spend, you can start to evaluate your habits. Usually people are surprised at how quickly little things add up – a coffee every day before work could add up to as much as $50-80 per month! Use a pink highlighter to mark receipts or line items on things that are not necessary spending and add up the total you spent last month (or an average of the last three months).

You may also, like Sam, have spending that are you locked into because of contracts, such as high cable bills or hefty car payments. In these cases, meeting with a financial advisor or counselor could help you find ways to get out of these traps. Sometimes paying a fee to get out of a contract will save you money in the long run. Highlight your spending on obligations (anything with a contract) in yellow.

Next pull out a green highlighter and mark all the necessary spending you do each month. Groceries, rent or a mortgage payment, and gas might be included on that list. But don't think that the green items are off the hook – you need to evaluate your spending in these areas too. Do you need to move into a less costly housing situation? What are you buying at the grocery store that is making your bill run high (and possibly adding pounds to your waistline)? Can you downsize your car to get rid of that gas guzzler?

As you track your expenses, make sure to account for every single penny of spending for at least a month. I have often seen people bring me their bank statements or receipts thinking they tracked all their spending, only to discover that a few items fell through the cracks. You need the full, accurate picture of your spending in order to move forward.

Make A Budget

Once you have tracked your spending for at least a month, you are ready to begin formulating a budget. Add up the total spending you had for the last month (expenses) and then compare that with your total income. How close or far apart those numbers are to each other will determine how much change you need to make to your spending habits.

When you make a budget, you begin with your income. You cannot create a budget based on what you spend now because chances are you do not earn enough to maintain your lifestyle. And remember, the primary goal is not to earn more. The goal is to place your heart and budget in line with God's heart for you. Spending more than you make communicates that you do not believe God has provided enough for you.

Once you have written down your income at the top of the page, you begin to write down spending in order of necessity. It is tempting to skip tithing in this process because you feel you do not earn enough to tithe. Challenge this thinking by reminding yourself that all you have belongs to God already. Check your values system – do I believe that what the Bible says is true? Do I believe God has my best life in mind? If so, can I take a step of faith in putting ten percent for God on the very first line?

Next begin to write housing expenses and other necessities, keeping in mind that these numbers could be trimmed down as we discussed earlier. See how far you get in writing expenses until you have reached the income number at the top of the paper. Don't forget to include saving in your budget even if you have not been saving already. A little each month can go a long way and can prevent chaos later.

Look at the list of items that did not make it into the budget. Can you live without these things? Can you redefine the words *need* and *want*? What steps do you need to take to trim down or re-prioritize? As you work through these issues, go back to chapters 4 and 5 to remind yourself about how to approach the process of change.

PAY DOWN DEBT

As I mentioned at the start of this chapter, I was raised on budgeting and often listened to Christian radio's Larry Burkett with my mother. (Keep an eye out for his books listed at the end of this chapter.) "Debt-free living" is a common theme for Christian money management and is a concept worth embracing. Bottom line: if you don't have it, you don't spend it.

Chances are that if you have had problems with money management you have incurred some debt. Our case example, Sam, has $20,000 of credit card debt plus his mortgage and car payments. He is almost functioning as a middleman in his own life, his money merely passing through his fingers from his employer to his creditors.

The first step in paying down debt is to stop incurring more. Cut up those credit cards! Switch to cash for a while and use an envelope system to set aside specific amounts of money for budget categories. Buying things you can't afford on a credit card with a high interest rate is like attaching 20-30% extra onto the price tag of your purchases. You are getting ripped off!

Once you have stopped adding to your debt, you can begin to make a plan to pay it down. Congress passed a law within the past few years that requires credit card companies to tell you how long it will take you to pay off your debt if you only pay the minimum payment each month. Check your statements or call the company to find this number (chances are it is a very long time from now). As you make your plan, do not simply look at the minimum payment required as this will add to the length of your loan and increase the amount of interest you pay.

Next prioritize your debt based on interest rate. If your car loan is at a 12% interest rate and your credit card is at 28%, pay off that credit card fast! Sometimes debt consolidation can help you lower your interest rates and make a payment plan. Look for a reputable credit counseling agency to help you, but beware high agency fees or taking out loans (more debt) to pay off your current debt.

FURTHER RESOURCES

We are certainly not short of resources on the topic of Christian money management. From the greats like Larry Burkett and Dave Ramsey to group study guides like Good Sense, you will find a book that fits your specific needs. You may even find that your church or one near you offers a financial management class or seminar. Having someone personally guiding you through the process of change can sometimes mean the difference between success and failure.

Here are some titles to get you started:
- *How to Manage Your Money* (2002), *Debt-Free Living: Eliminating Debt in a New Economy* (2010), *The Family Budget Workbook* (1993), and *Money Matters* (2001) by Larry Burkett
- *The Total Money Makeover* by Dave Ramsey (2009)
- *Good Sense Budget Course* (designed for a group) by Dick Towner and John Tofilon (2002)
- *Rich Christians In An Age of Hunger* by Ronald Sider (2005)

You can also check out *www.daveramsey.com* to find information on his Financial Peace University. On your smartphone, search for money management apps such as Mint or a variety of expense trackers or debt managers. Along the way, beware of books – Christian or otherwise – that have themes like "becoming a millionaire" or "fastest ways to get rich." These kinds of books are likely to bring you back to a focus on wanting more rather than on living within your means.

9

Addictions

As I mentioned in chapter 1, you should not skip over our sections on addictions just because you do not use drugs or alcohol. Those addictions are significant, but they are not the only form of addiction. Obsessive and addictive behaviors can often go undetected when they connect to food, shopping, technology, or sex. Read this chapter with an open mind to really examine your life for any addictions that may be present.

In our American society, some kinds of addictions go unnoticed because deviant behavior is widely accepted. Obesity is commonplace in our country, redefining "normal" and causing many to overlook a very real food addiction. Materialism is rampant, with most households carrying at least a few thousand in credit card debt. This norm fosters denial in those with shopping addictions. Technology has become an extension of ourselves, often controlling our behavior to the point of obsessive fixation. And sexual deviance of all sorts are widely celebrated in our culture and in the media, giving way to an "anything goes" attitude rather than an honest look at the self.

Before we jump into specific skills to overcome addiction in your life, I want to make sure you have really taken time to examine your life. If you have life chaos, it is quite likely you have found ways to cope with stress that are unhealthy and possibly addictive.

Ask yourself the following questions, writing down an honest answer for just you and God to look at.

- How many drinks of alcohol have I had in the last week? In the last month?
- How many cigarettes have I had in the last week?
- How many times did I abuse prescriptions or use illegal drug in the last week?
- How many times per day do I check my phone or computer for email/social media?
- How many hours did I spend video gaming in the past week?
- Have I looked at pornography in the last week? In the last month?
- When I go shopping, do I feel a rush of adrenaline?
- Track your eating for a day or two. How much did I consume that was unhealthy or empty calories? How often do I eat as a

response to stress? Do I find myself fantasizing about food?
- Are there any "bad habits" that I have thought I should cut back on?
- Has anyone in my life expressed concern to me about my behaviors, addictions, or bad habits?
- Have my health, mood, job, and/or relationships declined as a result of my behaviors?

Any habit or behavior that you cannot easily stop by yourself could be an addiction. I'm not talking about your *opinion* about whether or not you could stop. (This is often clouded by denial.) I am talking about habits you actually stop for a period of time. If there is anything in your life, TV and devices included, that you could not fast from for one month, you may be dealing with a life-controlling problem.

In order to take back control in this area of your life, there are some important steps you can take. We'll be referring back to Jimmy, our addictions case example from chapter 1, so be sure to go back and review his story. Let's take a look at four essential skills now.

FIND THE ROOT

We devoted a whole chapter earlier in the book to finding the root of your chaos problems. As we seek to remove addictive behavior from our lives, we need to go back to this root. Most addictions or bad habits come from an effort to cope with unpleasant feelings. We seek escape from the stresses or pain of life and find solace for a while in something that feels good.

Most people don't set out to become addicted to something. Jimmy, our case example, started out simply enjoying his video games. He played them for fun, without any notion that they could take over his life. The problem began when Jimmy started to use video games as a way to unwind after work. Red flag! He no longer simply had occasional fun with a video game. He had begun a *relationship* with his video games. Jimmy inadvertently put video gaming in a place in his life that he started to *need*.

I am not saying that coping or a need for escape is bad. In the next section we will specifically discuss ways to use coping skills to overcome addictions. We all need to de-stress sometimes. But if you are so stressed you need to escape daily, there is a deeper root issue going on. What in your life is creating a need such frequent escape?

The root issues you identified earlier on this journey will be helpful to go back and re-examine. Trying to escape your life chaos through addictive, life-controlling behaviors is only going to make your life worse. Getting some of the other areas of your life in order may decrease your need for relief. Pause and take time to write in your journal, asking yourself, "What feelings or parts of my life am I trying to erase using addictive behavior?"

Use Healthy Coping Skills

As I stated earlier, coping is a necessary part of life. We all experience stress, even if your life is fairly well-managed and in order. Our bodies were designed for rest one day out of seven, and God created the world for His and our enjoyment. Stepping into a place where you find legitimate rest in your life is critical to eliminating addiction.

If addictive behaviors are part of what defines *unhealthy* coping, how do we define *healthy* coping skills? I would argue that anything that benefits your mind and body would fall into a category of healthy coping skills. This includes activities such as exercise, spending time with encouraging friends, enjoying worship music, engaging in hobbies like painting or woodworking, praying, reading, or gardening to name a few. There are literally thousands of activities from which you could choose, and certainly too many to fully list here.

Think about positive activities or hobbies you have enjoyed in the past. Is there a way to enter back into these? What holds you back from enjoying these "escapes" that build your life up rather than destroying you?

Often when people seek to deal with addiction, there is a real sense of loss. This is because, as I mentioned with Jimmy, you have developed a form of relationship with your addiction of choice. You are trying to say goodbye to something that has brought you comfort and solace in your life. Initially, very few things will replace what you have lost. But it is possible to begin to replace destructive behavior with healthy coping skills.

Begin by making a list of healthy options to try. It might be sipping on a favorite tea or taking time to sit and read a book. As you engage in that activity, practice mindfulness by being aware of your thoughts and feelings in that moment. Intentionally step into enjoyment as you engage. These positive replacements will not satisfy you fully right away, but over time you will come to rely on these healthy habits to keep you emotionally on track.

PRACTICE DAILY SELF-CARE

Along with positive coping skills to manage stress, you also need to practice daily self-care. While there is certainly overlap between coping and self-care, it is important to distinguish the two. Self-care involves meeting your body's basic needs daily regardless of how stressed you feel. Coping comes in to provide additional emotional balance when you need it.

We discussed self-care when we talked about systems in chapter 2. Take time to review that section for a checklist on creating a good self-care system.

There are many reasons people neglect self-care. They may simply be unaware of their own needs. Or they may resist admitting that they have physical limitations. Others may feel that they are not worth taking care of.

Again the root issues you uncovered earlier will help here. What has held you back from daily self-care? What are some ways to begin to accept your limitations or begin to care about yourself?

Self-care is critical for recovery from addictions because your physical body has been harmed in the addictive behavior. Taking care of your body will generally decrease the amount of stress you feel, making your addictive behavior less "needed" in your day. Your body also needs a reset button, a sort of detox (formal or informal) to get back on track. Once your body is back on track, maintenance is key. Keep doing what has helped, rather than falling into a trap of thinking you feel good enough to stop healthy living.

INCREASE YOUR SUPPORT

You cannot beat your addiction alone. This is, in part, because honesty with at least one other person is critical to breaking through denial and facing yourself. Admitting to someone else the details of your addictive thinking and behaviors will help you see where you have gone off track.

Accountability is also critical to healing from an addiction. If you stop your addictive behaviors for a period of time and then you find yourself relapsing or having cravings, you need someone to talk to. You need someone to give you that loving "kick in the pants" when your thinking is wrong. And when you start neglecting your self-care and healthy coping skills, you need someone who knows you well to point it out to you.

You are not alone in fighting addiction. There are many who have gone before you, many currently struggling, and many who will come after you. Being part of a support group, having a sponsor, and sponsoring others are all ways to stay in touch with this reality. Hearing the story of someone who has been sober for three days can be a very useful reminder of where you have been and why you don't want to go backwards. And sharing your success could be the inspiration for someone else.

There are all kinds of support groups available regardless of your specific addiction. Celebrate Recovery is a Christian program offered at many churches for people dealing with a variety of addictions. The 12-step groups such as Alcoholics Anonymous, Narcotics Anonymous, Overeaters Anonymous, and Sex/Love Addicts Anonymous are widely available. Check out the next section on resources for a list of websites for online and in-person groups.

As we discussed in the introduction to this book, truly experiencing freedom in your life is not possible without a relationship with Jesus. In addition to human supports, focus on your recovery on your dependence on God. Surrender your desires to Him and let Him lead your life. Connect with the Bible and with a local church. Open your heart to healing from the inside out.

Further Resources

You can find out more about overcoming addiction in your life by browsing the self-help or recovery sections of your local book store. You can also check out these titles to get you started:
- *The Twelve Steps For Christians* by Friends in Recovery and RPI (1994)
- *Every Man's Battle* by Steve Arterburn et al. (2009)
- *The Life Recovery Bible*, NLT (2005) and *The Life Recovery Workbook* by Steve Arterburn and David Stoop (2007)
- *Gods at War: Defeating the Idols That Battle for Your Heart* by Kyle Idleman (2012)

In addition to printed resources, also be sure to check out online and local support options such as these:
- christians-in-recovery.org
- celebraterecovery.com*
- alcoholicsvictorious.org*
- aa.org*
- na.org*
- slaafws.org*
- oa.org*

These websites allow you to search for in-person meetings in your area.

Don't embark on a recovery journey by yourself! Read, share, and listen to others as you seek to take back control and overcome addiction in your life. Humbling yourself to be honest with God, honest with yourself, and honest with others is the first step in a life of healing.

10

ACHIEVING LIFE GOALS

Do you have dreams and goals for your life but you just never seem to be able to reach them? Do you feel like the odds are stacked against you so that every time you try to take a step forward you fall down? Your life goals seem like a fantasy: something you can dream about but you know deep down will never happen.

If you have had difficulty achieving life goals, you are likely to find at least one other area of chaos in your life. Maybe a relationship in your life is holding you back, or perhaps your finances are an obstacle preventing your from getting to your dreams. Or maybe you are in a decent routine that you just can't seem to move beyond. It's not destroying your life, but it's not getting you anywhere either.

Our case example for problems with life goal achievement (see Chapter 1) was George Bailey from *It's a Wonderful Life*. If you are not familiar with the movie, re-read the description we had in the first chapter. (Or better yet, go watch the movie – it's great!) George's life was mostly stable, with a bit of chaos. He had a falling down house he was trying to repair constantly, he had a big family with lots of hustle and bustle, and he had stress at work. But overall his life was fairly manageable, except for one thing: he could never escape the small town he longed to leave behind.

What are your life goals? What areas of chaos in your life keep you from reaching these? Are there other feelings, like fear or self-doubt, plaguing your mind? Do you have a sense of purpose, or a sense of what God has called you to do?

Some readers will have an answer to every one of those questions. They know where they want to be but just can't get there. Others of you may have no idea even what general direction your life should be headed. Purpose is fuzzy, a calling is a mystery. No matter where you fall, let's dive into four key strategies for developing and achieving life goals.

Know Yourself

Self-awareness is essential for all of life management, but it is especially important when setting life goals. Knowing your strengths and weaknesses, your patterns, and your purpose will propel you forward on a life mission. A lack of a proper understanding of yourself will immobilize you.

The first step in knowing yourself is done within the context of your relationship with God.

This means avoiding two extremes: "I am all set on my own" and "I am totally worthless." Neither of these statements are true about you. You are desperately in need of saving – if you haven't grasped that by now go back to the introduction of this book. You also have tremendous value and purpose because God has created you.

Once you have set yourself in a right relationship with God, you can start by simply observing yourself. What are your preferences? What skills do you have? What do you strongly dislike doing? What would it look like for you to take one step forward in your life right now?

George Bailey was unaware of the fact that he needed saving until his guardian angel showed up and jumped off a bridge to prevent George from committing that same act. Upon his arrival, the guardian angel began to show George what life would be like in the town if he had never been born. Through this very unusual kind of self-observation, George was able to understand himself better.

It is unlikely that a guardian angel will show up at your doorstep trying to get his wings. But you can observe yourself nonetheless. Carry your journal with you for an entire day and write down observations about yourself. What did you eat? Who did you talk to? What moods were you in? What did you enjoy? What did you not enjoy?

Feedback from others in your life can help you increase your self-awareness too. Ask friends, family, or a pastor to help you evaluate your strengths and weaknesses. Make sure you are ready for all they might say, and make sure the people you ask have a history of lifting you up and encouraging you. If a person has torn you down or burst every bubble you've ever had, don't talk to them about your life goals!

All of the data you gather on yourself can reveal a lot that you may have never noticed about who you are and what God has made you to be. The more data you gather, the more informed you can be while developing life goals. You can also take some personality tests as another source of data. See the end of this chapter in the section on further resources to learn more about personality tests you may want to take.

BE REALISTIC

In chapter 5 we talked about ways to develop a goal, including setting a realistic goal. There we were specifically addressing habit changes, but the same concept applies for setting life goals. Having one clearly articulated goal that is achievable (even if it takes 20 years!) will help you focus in on getting there.

Being realistic doesn't mean you don't dream big. In his book, *The Circle Maker*, Mark Batterson talks about dreaming big and praying hard prayers. At the end of the book, Batterson shares his own personal list of life goals. He's not playing around! But each goal is specific and individually listed, and my guess is that he has formulated short- and long-term plans for how to reach those goals.

So how do you know if your goal is realistic? In part, the first step of knowing yourself will tell you. If my goal is to be a major league baseball player, but I have never been on a team and only sort of know how to play, it's not realistic! The same is true for ministry goals. I have heard many people talk about their dream to go into full-time ministry (a very glamorized version of "ministry" by the way), yet they are not able to be consistently involved in serving in their local church. If you are not willing to start small, you will not accomplish big things.

Another reality check for life goals is to evaluate whether or not your goal involves gaining fame, money, or power. These three specific motivations are often a driving force behind an unrealistic goal. Yes, there are some people out there who become rich and famous. But that it is a rare event, and even when it does occur it often destroys a person's life emotionally and spiritually.

Finally, as you evaluate your life goals, begin to map out a basic plan for how to get there. If you want to be a doctor, you'll have to go to medical school. If your goal is to buy a house, you'll need a steady job and good credit. Are you willing to take the steps needed to reach your goal? Medical school is certainly no picnic. Working a steady job can be boring or frustrating sometimes. Evaluate whether or not the steps to reach your goal are something you are willing to work through even when the going gets tough.

Know Your Motives

As you took a look at whether your goals were realistic, you began to ask some questions of motive. Power, fame, and money are not good motivations because they are unlikely to happen, and you will probably quit when these do not materialize quickly. If you want to reach your life goals, you need to know your motives. What is going to keep you going when you want to give up?

Spend some time thinking or writing about the person you hope to become. *Identity* is the key word here. If your goal is to buy a house, then your hope is to be a *homeowner*. If your goal is to travel, you really want to become a *traveler*. What identity are you seeking to gain?

Clarifying your sense of identity can help you define your motives. Why do you want to become a traveler, for example? In the case of George Bailey, he wanted to become a traveler because he wanted to see himself as someone who was adventurous. This identity in his mind carried with it ideas of being a free-spirit with nothing holding him back.

Now let's use the same strategies we discussed earlier when we were exploring root issues. Why is George's ideal-self one in which he is a free-spirit with no responsibilities? The root issue here is that at least in part, he resents being the oldest who carries the family responsibilities. It was a role he never asked for and never wanted. He viewed this role as dull and even suffocating. He has problems in his family, social, and self-care systems.

Are you starting to see why understanding your motive is important? For George, his motive was to escape something in his life. Instead of fixing his systems, he wanted to run from them. At the root, he had unmet needs (freedom to be his own person and be a child rather than carrying adult responsibilities at a young age), and his life goals were actually his way of trying to resolve his root issues.

You will not accomplish your life goals if the main motive is to run away from your current life. Changing your systems, dealing with your root issues to find healing, surrendering yourself to God, and steadily moving forward one step at a time will make your goals succeed.

Once you have made sure your motives are not to run away from your problems, you need to write down what your motives are. Clear motives can be easily stated and written on an index card in a word or a sentence.. Sometimes you can even use a picture, like a photo of your child, as a reminder of your motivation. I would suggest identifying three clear motives for what you want to achieve any life goal. Carry photos or written motives with you or hang them where you will see them regularly. In this way you will have constant reminders of why you are working so hard.

Find A Mentor

Nothing is more critical to accomplishing your life goals than having a mentor who can give you feedback and cheer you on along the way. A mentor is not simply someone you look up to, but rather someone with whom you engage in a specific and defined relationship. Ideally a mentor should be someone who has accomplished some of what you hope to accomplish. For example, if you want to start your own business, your mentor should be a successful business owner.

When looking for a mentor, you want to evaluate the whole person. Take a look at their spiritual, emotional, and physical health. Assess whether or not they are someone you would aspire to become. If you are not sure, try to look for fruit in the mentor's life: what good is being produced?

Next comes the hard part: asking. You cannot have a mentor if you have never asked the person to become one for you. Mentoring is a formal relationship with boundaries and clear expectations. Decide how often you are asking your mentor to meet with you. Will they be available to you 24/7 or will you simply meet once a month for coffee? Are there specific topics you want to discuss, or a book you want to go through together? Or do you just want someone to be a sounding board?

Be prepared that the first one or two people you hope will be your mentor may say no. People are busy, and finding a good mentor takes hard work and perseverance. Don't take their refusal personally and don't give up. Once someone does agree to mentor you, be sure to stick to the boundaries you set from the beginning. It may also be a good idea to establish a length of the relationship from the start. Planning an end date (perhaps six months or one year) gives you both the chance to have an out if you need one.

FURTHER RESOURCES

There are a quite a few resources out there for you as you think about accomplishing your life goals. In general, you want to think about resources that will help you understand yourself better, help you form habits that can help you persevere on long-term goals, or give you ideas for a mentoring relationship.

Here are a few I've compiled for you as a starting point:

- *Living Life On Purpose: Discovering God's Best For Your Life* by Lysa TerKeurst (2000) – geared towards women
- *The 7 Habits of Highly Effective People: Powerful Lessons in Personal Change* by Stephen Covey (2013)
- *The 15 Invaluable Laws of Growth: Live Them and Reach Your Potential* by John Maxwell (2012)
- *How Successful People Think: Change Your Thinking, Change Your Life* by John Maxwell (2009)

- *S.H.A.P.E.: Finding and Fulfilling Your Unique Purpose for Life* by Erik Rees (2008)

You can also search for free online personality tests such as the *Myers-Briggs*. As of this book's publication date, this site is one option: *http://www.celebritytypes.com/test.php*. There are also personality test apps for your smartphone.

When you have taken time to know yourself, set realistic life goals, know your motives, and find a mentor, you will have far more success in accomplishing your life goals. Ordering your life around your goals means that each day you are asking yourself, "What one small step can I take today that can get me just a little closer to my goal?" Many distractions will come into your life and letting go of your goals will often be the easier course of action. (I have often thought that my life would have been a whole lot easier if I had never decided to write a book!) Keep on course and commit to fully become the person God made you to be.

11

Maintaining Your Victory

Imagine for a moment that you are running a marathon. You are about to cross the finish line and there is a huge crowd cheering you on. Raise your hands in victory (mixed with a bit of exhaustion) and know that right now you are crossing a major finish line! If you have applied this book to your life as I suggested in the preface, you have embarked on a tremendous journey of transformation.

Life, however, is unlike a marathon in that you have to keep running. Take time to celebrate the little successes as you succeed in making changes in your life, but don't forget that those changes will need maintenance. A life of order can quickly dissolve back into chaos without ongoing work.

The good news is that *maintenance* really just means that you need to keep doing what you've already started doing. Once you have understood your root issues, established healthy routines and habits, and have increased your supports, you have done the hard work. If you continue to do what you've been doing every single day, you will not be easily shaken.

The bad news is that life does not flow smoothly. As you take spiritual and emotional steps forward, there is a very real enemy seeking to knock you down and undo these changes. Stress, relationships, and old comfortable habits can creep in and challenge your new life.

There are two critical parts to maintaining your victory: *taking one day at a time* and *noticing red flags*.

A few years ago there was a bank commercial that described the millions of checks that the bank processed each year. The bank president said, "Processing all those checks is not about handling millions of checks well. It is about handling one check accurately, and then repeating that process millions of times." That statement describes so well what the orderly life is like. It is not about figuring out the thousands of days you likely have left on the earth. It is about figuring out how to live one day well and then repeating that thousands of times.

Taking one day at a time does not mean being shortsighted or never planning for anything. It means that you focus your thinking on what part of the plan is meant for today and what part must be left for its proper day. Taking one day at a time means that you don't have to worry about having a habit you do the rest of your life, but you just need to focus on living well today. Jesus summed it up when He told us not to worry about tomorrow because "each day has enough trouble of its own."[16] Sorting out which troubles are for today and which are not for today can make your stress far more manageable.

Noticing red flags is also an important skill to help maintain your victory. Red flags are warning signs – a signal that something is out of balance. Going back to your root issue and writing down some of your old problem behaviors can help you create a list of red flags. Examples of red flags are things like, "I missed two planned workouts in a row," or "I thought about calling that friend who I cut out of my life."

The key to a good list of red flags is that they are far away from a crisis point. They are the *first* thing you'd notice if you were heading off track, not waking up one day realizing you are living in chaos again. A red flag should not be, "I can't remember the last time I did my healthy daily routine."

Red flags can also be events. Your behavior may not have changed, but an external trigger may require you to tighten up your routine. A work transition, a death in the family, running into an old friend from a negative time in your life, or an event that reminds you of something you have gone through in the past can trigger old thinking and behavior patterns.

---

[16] Matthew 6:34

"Unusual events" should be on your list of red flags.

When a red flag comes up, there are a few responses you can have that will help keep you on track. First, call up a sponsor, mentor, pastor, or counselor that is working with you and tell them what happened. Then take a look at your self-care plan and be vigilant in doing everything on that list without wavering. Also take some time to write in your journal and possibly re-read old entries if it is helpful to remember why and how you developed your skills for life management.

Now that you have finished this book, I want you to take time to write out a commitment to yourself. You can write this in your journal or right here in this book on the page I've provided. Write three reasons you are choosing to change your life, three new habits you are committing to do daily, and a short promise that you will never give up on yourself. When life gets hard, re-read this commitment to remind you to stick with the journey.

I also want to invite you to share your story with me. If this book has helped you change your life, I'd love to celebrate with you! Feel free to email me at *newhope@ecic.tv* to tell me about your victory and know that I am cheering you on. I have prayed for you as I have written this book and I continue to pray that God will be glorified in your life as you seek Him and seek wellness. May He restore you and bring order to your life each and every day.

My Commitment To Myself

Three reasons I am changing my life:

1.

2.

3.

Three habits I commit to doing daily:

1.

2.

3.

I, _____,
promise never to give up on myself.

Signature:

Date:

Notes

Notes

NOTES

NOTES

Notes

Notes

About The Author

Kristen Kansiewicz is the founder and director of New Hope Christian Counseling, established in 2005 as a service of East Coast International Church in Lynn, MA. She graduated with a Bachelor of Arts degree in Psychology from Wheaton College (IL) and a Master of Arts in Counseling from Gordon Conwell Theological Seminary. She has established the Church Therapy Model, integrating professional counseling services into the church setting. Kristen is also a published author, regularly contributing to Wyn Magazine (*www.wynmag.com*) as well as *Children's Ministry Magazine* from Group Publishing.

Kristen's blog can be found at *www.churchtherapy.com*

Made in the USA
Middletown, DE
16 June 2016